The Prince Still Smiled

Amazing love breaks through a Cambodian family's night of terror

A true story by
CARL LAWRENCE

Tyndale House
Publishers, Inc.
Wheaton, Illinois

LIBRARY OF CONGRESS CATALOG CARD NUMBER 78-73216
ISBN 0-8423-4879-4, PAPER
COPYRIGHT © 1979 BY CARL LAWRENCE.
ALL RIGHTS RESERVED.
FIRST PRINTING, FEBRUARY 1979
PRINTED IN THE UNITED STATES OF AMERICA.

"It could never happen here," said Chea, as he continued to make a living, plan for his children's future, teach a Sunday school class, pray before meals, and be a good Christian.

It could never happen here . . . but it did.

ONE

Chea Aim rolled over on his straw mat. Although morning must be near, his body cried out for rest. He lay staring into the darkness, his hands stretched out at his sides. Set in his high cheekbones, his brown eyes burned as he tried to penetrate the predawn darkness that separated him from the tin roof overhead. He had nailed that roof into place himself just before his marriage thirteen years ago.

The quiet was broken only by the irregular breathing of his wife, who lay beside him. After a long night of fitful tossing, she had finally been overtaken by sleep.

Chea brought both his arms up and placed his hands behind his neck. For most of his thirty-two years, this was the time of day he cherished most. He often went to sleep at night anticipating the particular moment when he would awaken, roll over, put his hands behind his neck, and meditate on things past and things present. Not that he was a sentimentalist. He didn't spend that special time dreaming of what he wished he could be or what he could redo. It was a time when, almost selfishly, he grasped the few short minutes he could claim as his own, untouched by others' words, thoughts, and interruptions. Chea was caught

5

up in the vacuum of silence, the passing of life from darkness to light. It was his time to ponder, to be sad or joyful, to talk without utterance to himself and to others. Sometimes as he lay there, in a world where only he lived, his small, tight lips would open in a smile.

This morning was different. His eyes hurt, no matter how much he massaged them with his fists. His legs ached. The rice balls and salted fish that Wife had especially prepared for supper lay in his stomach. The taste of fermented fish coated his tongue.

Sitting up, he slid across the small room to the window. Quietly, in order not to wake the others, with practiced precision he pushed the thatched window cover outward with one hand. Leaning forward, he used the other to adjust the piece of bamboo that held the light savanna grass window in a horizontal position. He sat back down, folded his feet under him, and looked into the darkness. He could feel the oppressive air which always came just before the monsoon. Worse than that, he also knew inwardly that throughout his village many other fathers were staring with burning eyes out of open windows into the darkness. They too were listening, thinking, some more frightened than others. This time was no longer his own. It had been invaded by hundreds of other staring bodies, beginning to sweat while still aching from sleepless nights. Physically and mentally exhausted, each one was trying to erase or make sense out of the events of the past days. Chea couldn't do so, and he doubted that anyone else could either.

The capital city of his country had fallen at 10:00 A.M., just two weeks ago. Before the radio went dead, rumors had begun to flow unabated, growing more lamentable with each telling. Men whom Chea had not seen in years would come into his jewelry store to pass on a rumor. Always there was a look on their faces asking Chea to tell them it wasn't true. But he knew no more than the rest. All he could do was take each rumor and attempt to strip it of its embellishments. There was no lack of material to ponder.

"The big cities are being evacuated. The sick, the old, the children, everyone is being herded into the countryside."

"Entire villages are being massacred."

"All teachers, intellectuals, and persons with more than a third-grade education are being killed."

"Money will buy you nothing. A bag of gold will not buy one spoonful of rice."

"Soldiers are being taken into the forests, stripped naked, and massacred. Only their clothes are brought back."

"I have an uncle who escaped," another would chime in. "He saw it with his own eyes. The tires of the truck that returned had blood-soaked mud almost to the rims."

"It is true. Women and children are being bayoneted."

Sipping tea, Chea would reject each story by reminding Clerk, who had worked with him for eleven years, that "rumor is a way of life for our people."

Before taking another sip, Clerk would look up from his cup of tea with a mixture of skepticism and hope. Then, his head back down, skepticism was the obvious winner. Chea would lean back in his chair, push an account book aside, and explain, sometimes in ponderous detail, how "our entire nation's history is one big rumor."

"Look at the school books we studied," he explained, gesticulating with both hands to emphasize his point. "They said we are here today because a prince dreamed that a spirit gave him a bow and arrow and told him to conquer the sea. He went to sea and met

7

the queen's troops who were ready for battle as well. When an arrow from the magic bow struck one of the defenders, the queen surrendered. The prince and queen then got married, and here we are."

"Yes," said Clerk, with his usual deference, again looking up from his teacup. "Here we are, and with no magic arrows." He lifted his cup, drained it of the last drop, and stood up to return to his gem polisher. After taking one step, he turned back to Chea and with a look of slight encouragement on his face and said, "But we do have a Prince." He returned to his machine, picked up a stone, and began quietly to polish it.

Chea hadn't convinced Clerk any more than he had convinced himself. Each day brought new rumors. Chea, instead of enlarging on the rumor, would comment again on his people's propensity for gossip.

One morning the talking ended. Chea and Clerk both noticed it at the same time. Conversations emanating from outside the shop, usually unnoticed, stopped in mid-sentence. Words trailed off into unintelligible mumbles. The loud haggling of the market-place was replaced by wordless fear.

Chea and Clerk looked at each other, simultaneously rose from their machines, and went to the window. Women were putting vegetables on the stands. Merchants stood transfixed behind their fresh fruits, fish, and scales. The two of them could see people looking and pointing toward the other end of the street. They pressed their faces to the small opening, but could not see what the others saw. Cautiously, as though they were afraid to break the stillness, they moved to the door and stared down the street. Chea's muscles tightened. He gripped the door with one hand and Clerk's shoulder with the other. "They're here!" he whispered.

Clerk drew a deep breath through his teeth, something he always did to indicate a matter of great concern. As they watched intently, sweat began to form and run down Chea's back. A small group of men in single file walked down the street. Looking neither left nor right, they moved closer to Chea's store. Their pace was neither military nor listless.

White, sweat-stained scarves were tied around their necks, breaking the visual monotony of long, stringy black hair blending into black, sweat-stained pajama suits. Some wore hair bands. Their car-tire clogs made little noise as they stirred up puffs of dust along the street.

Although the visitors had the street to themselves, they continued to walk down the middle in single file. Chea and Clerk moved from the door to a window where they felt less conspicuous. Like everyone else in the village, they wanted to see but not be seen.

"How many are there?" Chea whispered.

"I can't see for sure," Clerk replied. "Looks like about ten."

"Ten?" whispered Chea, looking down at Clerk, who was pressing his face harder against the window frame to get a better view. "You're right, only ten. Wait a minute. Here come two more," said Chea.

"Twelve," replied Clerk.

"Twelve is not very many," said Chea. "There are over four hundred in our village." He was already beginning to calculate the odds, matching what he saw with some of the rumors he had heard. "Twelve is not very many to control four hundred. And look at them," he said in a little higher voice. "Why, they're only kids, just kids. Twelve kids."

His moment of reassurance was cut short. "But look what the twelve kids are carrying." Clerk emphasized the word *kids* as he spoke.

For the first time Chea noticed what Clerk had already seen and he found it suddenly difficult to breathe. Slung around the shoulder of each of the

9

visitors, now walking directly in front of the store, was something he had read about but never seen. It was the most widely and viciously used terrorist weapon in the world, the Soviet AK-17 automatic. In that banana-shaped clip protruding from the belly of the weapon lay thirty death warrants waiting to be delivered. And if they wouldn't do the job, extending from the end of the gun was a bayonet that would.

Across the street and to the right was the village square, in the middle of which was a large white statue of the Prince. It stood ten feet high, hands outstreched, face wreathed in a benevolent smile. Engraved in gold at the base were the words: "The pain of their subjects, and not their own pain, is the sadness of kings." The square would often explode with firecrackers welcoming a new year, or hum with the chanting of priests to celebrate the harvesting of another crop. Now, without a sound, without chanting, the visitors turned and began to make their way toward the statue.

Chea grabbed Clerk's shoulder. "Look!" he whispered, pointing to the last man in the line of visitors.

"What? Look at what?" asked Clerk, pushing his head out a little farther.

"That one," whispered Chea. "I know him. I'm sure I do."

Clerk looked hard and long at the last man in the single file now turning into the square. "He looks vaguely familiar, but—" Clerk paused. "He looks like all the rest: The uniform, the shoes, the gun—"

Never taking his eyes off the visitor, Chea interrupted. "Remember? He used to be in my church class." Clerk shook his head, trying to recall. "I can't remember his name," Chea went on, "but he's the one who always had a big smile on his face. The boy who would smile even when talking about unpleasant things."

"Yes, yes," replied Clerk, "I think I do remember.

10

But," his voice changed, "he's not smiling now. He looks just like the rest."

"Maybe it's because he doesn't dare," said Chea.

Smiling One followed the rest of the visitors into the square. Without speaking a word they sat leaning against the statue of the Prince, cradling their weapons in their hands. They looked straight ahead. They had positioned themselves so that together they could see both sides of the street, as well as the entrance and exit to the village.

For five days the same ritual was performed. Every morning at 8:15 sharp, the crowds in the street ceased talking, and the visitors made their procession into the town. Chea and Clerk took their position inside the store. Several merchants carried cases of cold Coke and placed them near by, offering them to the visitors, indicating they could have them, but never speaking.

At dusk the visitors got up, and the procession out of town was repeated. The Coke remained untouched, hot from sitting in the sun. The people, as though on cue, silently began to close their shops and make their way home. No one ever went to the town square in the evening. Social contact ended, but not the rumors.

On the sixth day the villagers, trying to remain as inconspicuous as possible, still watched the visitors with apprehensive glances. Business was not going on as usual. Women came to the marketplace, one at a time, quietly purchased their food for the day, and left. There was no haggling, no laughing, no gossip.

No one was buying jewelry, but Chea didn't expect them to. Actually, he made his money not so much from the local villagers as from the Chinese merchants across the border. Once every month he made a journey, crossed over, spent the night in a hotel (or "motel," as he learned to call it), and sold his stones. During those trips he devoured stories about the outside world. He spent many nights reading international magazines, falling asleep sometimes at dawn with a head full of knowledge, a stomach full of food, and a pocket full of money from a good bargain.

Suddenly Clerk turned off the water that was spilling over his machine's grinding gear to keep it cool. He cocked his head and listened.

"What's the matter?" asked Chea, looking up for only a second.

"I thought I heard something, a loudspeaker."

"Maybe they've turned on the music from the record shop," said Chea, turning off his machine. Then they both heard it. It wasn't music, and it didn't come from the record shop.

The two moved cautiously toward the door and stuck just their heads out for a quick glance at the visitors in the square. They sat sullen, showing no signs of having heard anything, their weapons cradled in their laps, a case of unopened Coke sitting a few feet in front of them. Chea and Clerk strained and could pick out a few words.

"Sounds like someone's making a speech," said Chea as he moved to the window for a better view. "I can understand a few words." He repeated each one. "Leave . . . shops . . . families . . . east road . . ."

A truck was moving slowly down the street, the kind the local merchants used to transport their food to outlying marketplaces. No other vehicles were around. Like the visitors, the truck had the street to itself. On top were two loudspeakers. The message carried foreboding words. Chea and Clerk stood silent and listened.

"We have destroyed the enemy, but a few remain. Our brave soldiers are here to rout them out, and we do not want anyone to be injured. You are all to leave, close your shops, go home, get your families, and leave by the east road."

When the truck went by the shop, Chea could see two men in the front seat. They wore simple blue uniforms with sun helmets made of straw. One drove, and the other spoke into the microphone held close to his mouth, repeating the same little speech. As they passed the visitors in the village square, there was no sign of recognition among them.

For five days and nights this new invasion of the village continued. From early morning till late at night, the truck traveled back and forth, up and down the streets. Sometimes the voice cajoled. Some days the speaker reached a hysterical pitch. Other days the voice was almost apologetic, not pleading, not warning, just informing—a good soldier doing his duty. The people responded with traditional stoicism. They tried to shut it out of their homes and minds. The rumors were now replaced with little conversations, dwelling on the fact that these are our people and we do not kill each other; we are civilized; we are from one tree.

On the fourth day, the peacefulness of Chea's shop was broken by a booming voice. "Hello, brothers."

The greeting overrode the noise of Clerk's grinding machine. Both Chea and Clerk stopped working, frightened, and looked up.

In the doorway, blocking out the sun, was Colonel In Yean of the regular army. He was the commander of a small group of regular soldiers whose barracks were just outside town. The local citizens called them "the Colonel's children," because they averaged thirteen years of age, and none of them had ever seen a real war. They were put together on orders from the government at the capital to protect local villages. One of them was Clerk's fifteen-year-old son.

Both men got up from their machines and walked toward the door. Chea wasn't sure whether he was smiling because he was happy to see his old friend, or at the incongruity of it all. A bit overweight, the

13

Colonel stood, all six feet of him, resplendent in a new khaki uniform. The five gold stripes on his shoulder boards, the polished crossed cannons on the lapel of his blouse, his boots (which mirrored parts of the room), all were in sharp contrast to the other army that occupied the square.

Around his neck was the Colonel's trademark, a bright blue silk scarf. He was never without it. Some said he even slept in it. It had been given to him by the governor at the dedication of the statue under which the visitors now spent their days.

"Does that piece of silk really bring you good luck?" someone would ask with respect, awe, and sometimes jesting.

"Well," the Colonel would shout, "I still have a neck to wrap it around, don't I?" Everyone would laugh, but always with him, not at him.

The Colonel walked up to the counter as Chea went around to face him, and Clerk went to the window to see if anything was happening in the square. It wasn't. Visibly relieved, Clerk's smile became more genuine as he nodded to Chea that everything was all right.

For several minutes the Colonel and Chea exchanged polite greetings, though when you were with the Colonel you did the listening and he handled the greetings.

"Suppose you wonder what I'm doing here?"

"Well, yes, I am," replied Chea respectfully.

"I need a nice stone," blared the Colonel.

"What for?" asked Chea, and then quickly reached under the counter and brought out a blue bag loaded with stones he had been accumulating.

The Colonel looked at them and said in a hushed tone, "This has to be a very special stone."

"Why?" Chea asked. Clerk moved closer.

"Because," said the Colonel, turning around to see that no one was listening, "it's for our Prince."

14

"The Prince!" gasped Clerk.

"He's coming back to the capital, and I have been invited to be there to greet him."

"He's coming back! The Prince is coming back! You hear that?" said Chea, turning to Clerk who was standing so close to him that their noses almost touched.

"Shhh, not so loud," said the Colonel. "'It's still a top military secret." The Colonel signaled with his head toward the village square. "Even they don't know." The Colonel began to go through the stones with his manicured fingers, looking for one that especially appealed to him.

Chea stepped to his safe and took out a blue velvet bag. "Wait, Colonel. If this is for the Prince, maybe you should have this one."

Chea took out a large blue sapphire he had been working on for some months and set it down in front of the Colonel.

The Colonel, sucking air between closed teeth, showed obvious approval. He picked it up and gently turned it around, his chubby fingers rolling it from one hand to another. "But," said the Colonel, "this blue sapphire, this would be much too expensive."

Chea spoke quickly. "No, no, you must take it to the Prince as a gift from the village. It will cost you nothing."

"Oh, we can't do that," said the Colonel.

"You must," said Chea. He knew he wouldn't have to argue long. The Colonel hadn't risen in the ranks of the regular army without being a shrewd bargainer.

"Well, if you insist," said the Colonel, "but be assured I'll tell the Prince who gave it to him. Our village will be burned into his memory."

Clerk liked that idea and chimed in, "I helped cut it as well."

Chea said, "That's right, but remember, Colonel, it

is to come from the entire village, not just the three of us."

"Of course, of course," said the Colonel. "I'll take it as your personal envoy."

As the excitement of the moment subsided, Clerk moved back a few steps, suddenly becoming aware of the fact that he was facing an army colonel, and that this was not his shop, he was only the Clerk. But there was still something he wanted to ask. As Chea took the sapphire and began to wrap it, Clerk timidly approached the Colonel. "Sir," and he hesitated.

"Yes," the Colonel said, looking at a new cigarette lighter that was on display, and thinking he wouldn't be above accepting it as a gift—in case the Prince had an entourage.

"I am wondering, sir," Clerk said, "will you take your soldiers with you when you go? Will they go to the capital with you?"

"Of course, of course," said the Colonel with his usual exuberance once he realized that the conversation would not deal with money, his sapphire, or the lighter—which he now used to light a long cigarette, as though it were already his.

"Then, Colonel, my son will be going with you?"

"Ah, that's right, your son is in my army. Well, don't worry, he will be escorting me to the capital along with the rest of the troops."

"Thank you, sir," said Clerk with a sigh of relief. "I am glad. You see, he is my only son, my only child, for that matter."

Chea walked up to the counter and handed the sapphire, now enclosed in the blue velvet bag, to the Colonel. The Colonel opened the top pocket of his khaki blouse, put the sapphire in, and then rebuttoned it. "Well, I must hurry. The truck will be picking us up early tomorrow morning." He started for the door, and then turned. Taking the cigarette out of his mouth, he dropped it to the floor, ground it with his foot, and said almost as an afterthought, "Don't worry about them." He pointed with his chin to the village square. "The only thing they're going to use those bayonets for is to cut each other's hair." He laughed loudly as he walked out the door.

Chea and Clerk looked at each other with obvious relief. It was the first positive assurance they had had since the visitors came. Colonels don't spread rumors.

"It was worth the blue sapphire," said Chea, "just to get some news."

"Plus one cigarette lighter," Clerk added, looking amused.

That had been two days ago. Now, the sun was beginning to push the darkness to the other side of the world. Chea was not sure how long he had been sitting, looking out the window, reviewing the developments of the past two weeks, but the process had done little to alleviate his apprehension. He got up slowly and took the few steps back to his mat. Quietly he lay down beside his wife, who was lying on her back, sleeping more soundly than before. He hushed his breathing so as not to awaken her.

His mind went back to that day when he had spoken his first words to her. For several weeks he had secretly admired her. He saw her Sundays at church, and sat near the back just so he could watch her, dreaming that some day they would sit together. It was unforgivable to mention to a young lady her beauty, her figure, or her clothes, so, after he finally gathered the courage to speak to her, they talked about the weather, the beauty of the sky, the size and shapes of leaves on banyan trees. Then he sent her notes—and finally there was a visit from his father to her father's home to initiate formal procedures. Fortunately, unlike some of his young friends, he did not have to go to work first for his future in-laws to prove his worthiness. Nor did he have to pay her family what is called "the price of mother's milk": repayment for raising such a healthy daughter.

One year later they were standing at the front of that same church, with a foreign missionary binding them together as one.

On their wedding night he gave her a small white scarf. He had purchased it two years before, even before he dared speak to her about the "beautiful sky." After their engagement was announced, he was still too frightened to give the scarf to her. Now he mustered his courage, and with a blush that spread from his neck to the top of his head he told her how he had kept it all this time. She accepted it with tears, pronouncing the traditional words, "With this to fix the words and to tie the heart." And they became one.

Since then she had "crossed the Tongle Sap" five times. Three of the babies had survived. Though traditionally the mother handled the day-by-day care of the children, Chea never abdicated his authority as the "final word," whether in a major crisis or a childish squabble. It was Chea, not his wife, who had to enforce the rule that their children could not have nicknames. He was aware that such a practice had its root deep in the animism he so abhorred, and which he blamed for many of his country's problems. Children were named after astrological numerals or grotesque animals to frighten off evil spirits, but he did not countenance that form of exorcism. When his children were sick, the neighbors would advise him to change their names to confuse the spirit that was responsible. The spirit would then leave and the child would be healed. Though Chea believed in healing, he knew it didn't come from that source. And so his children's names stayed the same: Che Sok Khom, his twelve-year-old son, who was called, properly, Khom; a nine-year-old daughter, Che Sopha, called Pha; and two-year-old Chean Penh, whose bubbling personality and constant smile earned for her a name of endearment all were proud of: the title of Little Baby Sister.

Each of the children held a special place in the hearts of Chea and his wife. Sometimes he was too strict, sometimes too lenient, but always he tried to do what was best.

Khom was being groomed to replace him in the shop someday. Already Chea took him to work when there was no school, and often Khom told his father, as delicately as possible, that his schoolwork was interfering with his ability to learn how to shine sapphires. Chea took great pleasure in teaching Khom the art of his trade, from the digging of the stones to the selling. Several times a year they packed food and walked the day's journey up to the foothills where the sluggish mountain streams had transported the stones to the flat lands below. Khom spent hours watching the women workers make their way to the hillside with their empty buckets. There they filled them with the soft igneous rock, brown on the outside and slate-colored on the inside, and then carried the heavy load on their heads to the men workers. The men had built dams, forming pools about four feet in diameter, and sat in the middle of the pools, each holding a closely woven bamboo tray. The women dumped their buckets of dirt into the pool, and the men reached down with their trays and scooped it up. For hours they sat shaking the trays from side to side into the water. Soft muddy rock oozed out of the cracks. Again and again they repeated the process until finally only a few rocks remained. They cast skilled eyes upon them, threw some away, and stuck a couple of them into the folds of their *sampot*, always careful to let no one else see how big the stone really was, always cursing that it wasn't bigger. But everyone there knew that in the fold was a sapphire, ruby, white zircon, or some other precious stone waiting for skillful hands to give it life. Khom was anxious to learn his father's skills.

Chea's daughter Pha was like his wife. She had the same delicate features and reserved personality. Taught well by her mother, she rarely complained, was serious about her work, and took great pride in taking care of Baby Sister.

As often as possible, Pha would go with her mother to market—learning the art of haggling over prices, a practice exercised more as a form of social intercourse than for financial benefit. Not yet a teen-ager, Pha was unaware that she was sometimes being evaluated by matchmaking mothers. To help her, Pha's mother would always describe new acquaintances as "so-and-so's mother," so that Pha could do some evaluating of her own. She and her mother were inseparable, and when either was sick, the other would often come down ill in sympathy. Chea sometimes worried about what would happen if one of them died. Death was common, striking nearly every home at least once a year. A high infant mortality rate plagued the nation, and Chea drew comfort from the fact that Pha had reached nine. Now she was past the young children's diseases.

Baby Sister was the polished jewel of the family. Her good nature put the rest of the family to shame. She rarely cried, and was just at the age where she was beginning to imitate other people's talk. One of the first expressions she learned was "Daddy's home." Each evening, no matter how tired, how weighted down with problems he might be, Chea was revived by Baby Sister's call when he entered the yard. In a few seconds her chubby little legs would come down the front ladder, as she held on with equally chubby arms, hit the ground, and ran to be picked up. Daddy was home, and all the problems of the world suddenly dissolved into a steady stream of chatter.

As Chea lay on the mat, with the sun beginning to shine through the window, he realized that the very things about his family that gave him the greatest joy now caused him worry. The foreboding of the day hovered over him. How many times would he be able to wake up and find Wife beside him, comfortable in her sleep? Would his son ever take over the business? Would there be a business left? Would he get to see the day his daughter passed from childhood and adolescence on to motherhood? And would some catastrophe ever remove the sparkle from Baby Sister's eyes?

His brooding was broken by the sound of the loudspeaker coming down his street. What would the messenger be like today? Would he shout and scream, or would he simply pass on instructions?

As the truck got closer to the house, Chea heard a different voice.

His wife sat up in bed.

The messenger and the message were different. Chea and Wife exchanged anxious looks as a new and authoritative voice spoke to them from somewhere on the street. Roosters stopped crowing, and dogs stopped barking. They too seemed to listen with what Chea thought was a sense of impending disaster.

Slowly, distinctly, cutting each word at the end, the messenger repeated the message: "Attention, all citizens. Every man, woman, and child will meet in the village square at 10:00 A.M. This is important. Anyone who does not come will be dealt with severely. This is your final message." The truck rolled down the street, and the messenger started again. "Attention, all citizens . . ."

All three children came into the room.

"Did you hear, Father?" asked Khom. "We are to be

in the village square at ten o'clock for a very important meeting."

"I heard," said Chea, trying to add bravery to his voice.

"What are we going to do?" asked Pha.

"We will go the village square at ten, that's what we'll do." Chea stood up and reached for his towel. He had put a barrel of water on top of his house and connected a shower head to the bottom of it. He had draped palm fronds around it to give him privacy. As he walked out of the room the children gathered around their mother. Stepping onto the ladder, he turned and spoke with a trace of humor in his voice. "And what's more, we'll all go, and we'll be on time."

As he left he heard the two older children begin to ask Wife questions. In the shower, he pulled the cord and put his head under the cold water, trying to wash away the pain of the long night, hoping that the water would awaken him from a bad dream.

The sun began to penetrate the metal roof, making the three rooms in the house hot and steamy. No one complained. Chea tried to act as normally as possible. He explained that the new government probably wanted to conduct a census and this was the easiest way of doing it. He could see that only Baby Sister accepted the idea.

"Yes, the gubberdent want a con . . . con . . . a what, Daddy?"

Everyone took the occasion to laugh. Glancing out of the side of his eye, Chea saw tears come to Pha's eyes. His wife reached over, took her hand, and squeezed it. Khom stood up and said, "Well, I'm ready to be counted, so let them count." Though his bravado relieved some of the tension, their apprehension remained.

Chea and Wife decided that rather than an ordinary breakfast they would have a full meal, usually reserved for one evening a week. Certainly this would make the children forget the uncertainties that awaited them at the square.

As was always the case in Chea's home, eating was a ritual. He considered it a time of teaching and training, as tradition dictated. His father had done it, and now so did he.

The children smiled as Wife brought several different dishes with straw covers and placed them on the mat, which had been the parents' bedroom only a few hours before. This was not going to be an ordinary breakfast of rice, fish, and water, and they all showed their approval. One bowl was heaped with pork, a treat that always indicated a special occasion. Meals were usually not interrupted by talking, but this morning Chea began to ask the children questions about school and other subjects. He wanted to keep them from noticing that the chickens had stopped scratching under the house. The dogs were not nosing about. No vendors were ringing their bells up and down the streets. No women were yelling at each other from the doorways of their homes. No housegirls were comparing notes on last night's activities.

The family felt the silence. Was everyone else at home having one last meal? Chea wondered. Quickly he erased the thought from his mind, bowed his head, and prayed as he did at every meal. Then he said, "Well, let's not let this food go to waste." He reached over, took a large helping of pork, and put it into his bowl. He passed it to his son, then to Wife, Pha, and Baby Sister. It was a ritual that never varied, a constant reminder of the family responsibilities.

He picked up a piece of pork, admired it, and then dipped it into the bowl of *Tik-try*. The sauce, made of fermented fish oil, was used at all social levels from peasants to kings. He reached into the rice bowl and with his fingers took a ball of rice and placed it in his mouth, followed by the saturated pork. The rest of the family did the same. Attempts to continue conversation died at the end of each new sentence. They ate together solemnly.

When the food was gone, Chea picked up the bowl in front of him and took a mouthful of water. He ran the water around in his mouth, then swallowed it. Each member of the family did the same with their water, and in the proper order—even Baby Sister, who, though last in the hierarchy, usually did not miss the occasion to imitate her father by overacting the entire scene. A cold shiver hit Chea this morning as she picked up the bowl, drank a little of the water, and set it down without giggle or comment. Her action was not lost on the others. The quiet caused Chea to look at his watch and suddenly stand up.

"It's 9:30." Breakfast had taken longer than they expected. "Come, we can't be late. Let's hurry and get dressed," he commanded, trying to instill some confidence into the household.

Pha and her mother quickly picked up the dishes, took them to the area below the house where the food was cooked, and then returned to their rooms.

Chea and Wife were alone. He went to his wooden clothes closet, the only piece of furniture in the room, took out a key, and opened it. Ordinarily he wore a pair of trousers and a white shirt with long sleeves to work, but today was no ordinary day. He took out his *sampot*, a single ten-foot piece of fine cotton. Deftly he wrapped it around his waist, fastened it in front, and then let it fall to mid-calf. Stooping over, he picked up the other end, passed it between his legs, and tucked it in his waistband at the back. In front it looked like a pair of short trousers with flared cuffs. In the back it looked like a skirt. He put on a white shirt and slid a pair of imported leather thongs over his white socks. Wife took the cue and called to the children to dress as they would for church. She too put on a *sampot*, along with a blue blouse and a shawl she had made that week. "For some special occasion," she had said.

Chea watched as she went to a small box in one corner of the room. Taking a key from under the mat and bending down on one knee, she unlocked the box. She reached in, took something out, and tucked it into the waistband of her *sampot*. As she was putting her blouse back over the top of the *sampot*, Chea saw that she had taken the white scarf he had given her on their wedding night. He quickly left the room, admonishing everyone to hurry.

Khom had taken the ivory dove his father had carved for him and hung it outside his shirt, instead of leaving it inside as he usually did. It was a very special gift from a father to his son. Some of Khom's friends, who did not believe as he did, wore amulets around their necks: teeth from dead animals, a piece of bone, or any other object that would bring good luck. The important thing was that they were blessed by the local sorcerer, or *kru*, as she was known. Whenever Khom fell and hurt himself, his friends said it was because he wasn't wearing an amulet. As the other children got older, they went out on hunting expeditions, looking for animals they knew weren't there—and couldn't catch with their wooden spears if they were. But they wouldn't let Khom join them because he didn't have an amulet.

Many times Khom had come into the jewelry shop crying. His friends had all gone on an expedition, and he was left behind. He had nothing around his neck blessed by the witch doctor to protect him from evil spirits, they said.

One day, on a selling trip across the border, Chea purchased a small piece of especially fine ivory. He worked on it secretly for many hours. When he was finished, he had two shining objects which he hung on small chains. One was a small cross, the other a beautiful white dove. That night at supper Chea wore his cross, and one by one the family noticed it. He then explained the difference between it and the amulets that others wore. He could see the desire in his son's eyes. Then Chea presented Khom with the carved dove. Khom immediately put it around his neck and had never taken it off since. This morning he wanted everyone to see it. As they walked to the door, Chea reached under his shirt and took out his cross, to wear it in the same way. From the corner of his eye he could see that the action pleased his son.

The family made their way down the ladder to the ground a few feet below and gathered in a small circle at the bottom. Chea said a few words, they took each other's hands, and began to walk toward the village square. Several neighbor families came out of their houses and started to move in the same direction. Many of them also were dressed up as if they were going to a celebration. Usually, when meeting, the men would walk in front, with the women and then the children tagging along behind, followed by a couple of dogs, all wanting to be part of the celebration. This morning, the families stayed together. No one did much more than nod in recognition, and no dogs joined in behind. Silence, even more eerie than that accompanying a funeral, pervaded the entourage as they wended they way toward the city square.

In less than ten minutes they came to the main street, a block away from the square. Chea led his family past the shuttered storefront. The marketplace was deserted. As they walked, Pha took her mother's hand and began to weep quietly. "I'm frightened. Something is wrong. I'm frightened."

Chea moved over and put his arm around her. He could muster no words. The only difference between them was that he had been taught that frightened men don't cry. Baby Sister walked quietly alongside, ignoring the things that ordinarily would cause her to be picked up and carried the last few yards. Many people had already gathered in the square and were beginning to spread into the main street. Everyone was standing in front of the statue of the Prince, flanked by the visitors on each side and with two in front of the statue. Standing just to the right of the benevolent Prince was the one visitor whom Chea knew from his church class, the Smiling One. There was no trace of any emotion, or even life, on his face as he stared into the gathering crowd. Chea was certain that a dead man, propped up with his eyes open, would look the same.

The sun crept across the sky and beat down on the villagers. Children began to cry. Like the rest, Chea kept trying to swallow, craving a glass of water. His shop was less than twenty feet away, and inside were two thermos jugs of tea. Yet he dared not move. Together they stood, Chea with his wife beside him on one side and his son on the other. Pha stood directly in front of Wife, and Baby Sister stood in front of Chea, pushing herself into his legs, trying to get away from the statue but not wanting to leave her father.

Chea looked at his watch. It was 10:00 A.M.

A few seconds later a ripple was heard in the crowd. Feet shuffled on the dirt street as people parted to let someone through. A big man with a khaki uniform and a straw helmet made his way directly to the statue. The visitors continued to look into the audience. Again, no flicker of recognition passed among them. Smiling One took a few steps, picked up a microphone, and handed it to the stranger. The truck with the loudspeakers was parked directly behind the statue.

The stranger stood for what seemed minutes, but was really only a few seconds. He said nothing. He looked over to the far left and stared at the people, then moved his gaze across the entire assemblage. Chea was certain they had made contact as his eyes passed him, though the stranger gave no indication.

No one moved, no children cried. Silence hung over the square.

The stranger again looked out over the audience and pointed to a man a few yards in front of him. He motioned him to come forward. As the man started to move, the stranger spoke quietly, motioning for him to bring his family.

Chea recognized the even, steady voice. The stranger was the new messenger who had delivered the last message earlier that day.

Chea stood on his toes to see which family the stranger was pointing to. He recognized a fellow merchant, Keo Dara. He leaned over and whispered the man's name to Wife.

"Oh," she moaned quietly. "What is going to happen?"

Chea nudged her to be quiet. Baby Sister pushed deeper between Chea's legs, nearly pulling down his *sampot*. His son stood with his hands by his sides, his trembling knees betraying his attempt to hide his fear. Pha held onto her mother, her hands reaching around her mother's waist.

The stranger spoke a few words to Keo Dara, who now stood with his wife and their three children, a twelve-year-old daughter and nine- and four-year-old sons. Chea's wife knew the mother well. They had taken tea together many times.

The stranger motioned for them to stand in front of the smiling statue. They moved together, the parents in back, the children in front. It was apparent that Keo Dara's wife was about to "cross the Tongle Sap" for the fourth time. The family stood silently in front of the statue as though posing for a family picture. No one smiled. No one moved.

Chea stopped breathing. The stranger made an imperceptible motion to two visitors standing in front of the statue.

The air was filled with staccato machine-gun fire. Some people fell to the ground. Others screamed. The acrid smell of spent gunpowder began to waft over the villagers' heads.

"To your feet, all of you," shouted the stranger into the microphone.

Pha buried her face in her mother's bosom. Khom stood erect, both hands doubled into tight fists at his sides. Little Sister grabbed her father's leg. Chea reached down and stroked her hair. Her crying was drowned out by the stranger speaking into the microphone. "You will ignore our warning no more. Do not go home, do not go into your business. Turn, and leave town by the east road. The soldiers will lead the way."

When everyone continued to stand in stunned silence, he screamed into the microphone, "Move!"

Like one person, everyone began to move toward the east road that led out of town. As he turned, Chea glanced at the grotesque forms of the Dara family at the foot of the statue. The children standing in front had been shot first. Attempting to grab them, the parents too had been shot, and had fallen on top of the children. Chea's gaze moved up and he saw that blood had stained the hands of the benevolent stone Prince who still smiled across the square.

The liberation of Cambodia had reached their village.

TWO

Women's cries of anguish were mixed with fathers' admonitions to "hurry, or we may be next." Families instinctively joined themselves into small groups. Chea's wife quickly took the shawl she had made for some special occasion and wrapped it around her. She then picked up Baby Sister and placed her on her back, the child's body resting inside the saddlelike shawl.

Chea gently took Pha and pried her away from her mother. She wept uncontrollably. He lifted her frail body, and her arms wrapped tightly about him as she buried her face in his neck. Chea patted her back, wishing for the long nights when her only problem had been a bad stomachache.

The family turned and started the slow walk down the main street which would soon become the east road. Slightly ahead of them, Khom walked erect with his hands still doubled into tight fists at his sides. His knees still shook.

An elderly woman stood transfixed staring at the statue. Chea took her arm and began to lead her along. Suddenly she broke away and, with a cry that sounded like a wounded animal, began to run in the opposite direction. A burst of gunfire violated the air. Without looking, Chea knew that she would never walk down the east road.

A man whom Chea knew only by sight ran up to him, took him by the shoulder, and cried out, "My wife, she is at home. She is about to have a baby, but I can't go to her. What will I do?" A soldier moved in beside them with one quick plunge of his bayonet. The man's question had been answered for him. He would do nothing but fall down dead at the soldier's feet.

Chea's wife leaned against him. "I can't go on," she said. "I'm going to faint." He freed one arm from around Pha and stuck his hand between her back and Baby Sister. They began walking east. If she fell, she would not be allowed to get up again. He pleaded with her, trying to keep his voice steady.

Khom dropped back a couple of paces, took his mother's other arm, and placed it over his shoulder. "Lean on me," was all he said. It was a transfusion of courage. She moved forward with the rest of the people.

"Let's try to walk a little faster," said Chea, noticing that they were closer to the back of the group than the front. "Let's stay in the middle as much as we can and remain inconspicuous. We'll be less apt to get hurt." It was a trait Chea had. He called it humility, but now he wasn't sure that humility was the right word.

The family picked up their pace and soon were in the middle of the group, not far enough to the front to be a leader, not far enough back to be a straggler. A safe position.

Were they like old water buffalo being herded away when they could no longer be of any use, heading for the slaughterhouse? Or were they like the younger stock, being sent to the countryside to pull plows, walk through the mud, and forever be beasts of burden? Chea drew in his breath, hoping for another option: a green grazing pasture.

Wife had now regained her strength, and Khom moved from his mother's side over to his father. Without looking up, and barely moving his lips, he spoke. "There are only twelve Khmer Rouge, and at least four hundred of us. Why don't we rush them?"

"I have already thought of that," said Chea. "There are twelve of them. Each weapon has thirty bullets. That means that three hundred and sixty would die just from the guns alone, and then there are the bayonets."

"But," interrupted the son, "at least some of us would survive. We wouldn't all have to die."

"The price would be too high,"

"But still, some would survive."

"It's not just the deaths I'm thinking of," whispered Chea. "Revenge is not to be taken by us."

"We aren't caribou," hissed Khom. He must have been reading Chea's mind. "I don't want revenge," Khom continued. "I just want to make sure that Mother, Pha, and Baby Sister get away from here and make it across the border to Thailand."

"We will discuss it later," said Chea, noticing one of the soldiers nearby.

"Later," said Khom, "yes, later, after we are all dead."

Chea was shocked at the hostility in his son's voice. He had never heard him speak that way before. The soldier, now parallel to him, prevented him from admonishing Khom and reminding him that he was still his father and the one to decide when and where they would attempt to escape. His son again moved over to his mother's side, again taking her arm and placing it on his shoulder.

Bursts from AK-17's, interrupting screams, pleas of mothers, cries of elderly persons running until a bullet caught up with them, the ominous silence following the glint of a bayonet in the hot sun, all these accompanied the remaining villagers as they moved down the road.

The sun was now directly overhead. Chea had lost count of how many times he had heard the short staccato of an AK-17, how many times he had heard his son say, "They only have three hundred bullets now . . . 296 . . . 291."

Chea's arms ached from carrying Pha. He whispered into her ear that it was time she walked a little, that he couldn't carry her unless he got some rest. Her only response was a frightened cry and a tightened grip. Finally, with some persuasion, she loosened her arms and began to slide slowly down his front as he continued to walk. Suddenly Chea's sandal caught on a stone and he tripped. Letting out a scream, Pha fell from his arms and lay sprawled in the dust. People moved aside. Without warning, a Khmer Rouge stood over her with his bayonet. It was the Smiling One. Still on his knees, Chea moved quickly, covering the few feet that separated him from his daughter. He looked up into the Smiling One's eyes. Time froze. Smiling One moved his bayonet to the side and prodded an older man in the buttocks. The old man was wearing only a pair of short pajamas, and blood began flowing down his bare leg. He screamed, raised both hands in the air, and, half running, half limping, rushed forward.

Chea picked up Pha, stiff with fear, and again held her. They continued their walk. No one seemed to notice what had happened. Everyone just kept moving down the east road as the sun moved from its apex.

Chea was troubled. He did not curse himself for stumbling or dropping his daughter. Rather, a nervousness crept into his mind as he realized that no one had offered to help. There was not even a look of pity on the faces of those who moved by.

"That is one reason all this is taking place," he thought to himself. His mind raced back a couple of years before, when many of the families had gone down to the river to swim. A young girl about Pha's age had brought her baby sister. Although neither of them could swim, they suddenly found themselves in water over their heads. The older girl made her way to shore, but the little one was fighting to keep above water. The older girl screamed to the more than fifty people standing by, pleading for someone to save her sister. None moved. The older sister ran home to get help and in a few minutes was back with her father. She pointed to the spot in the water. Others pretended not to be there. The father waded in, reached down with one move, and scooped out the body of his little girl. By this time the mother and grandmother had arrived. They fell on their knees on the riverbank and began to call the little girl's name. Later they were seen building a fire and putting banana leaves on it. They laid the child's body on the leaves, hoping that if they warmed her body, she would come back to life. She never did.

That night when Khom told his parents what had happened, Chea was greatly disturbed. But he didn't want to place any blame, and the issue was never again discussed. Had he been there, he was sure he would have rescued the child. That incident had been buried in Chea's mind, but now it came back to him. He wondered if retribution was not a reality, after all. Not revenge, just justice.

The exodus was now about four hours old. People were vomiting while walking. Others were moving as though they were already dead. They couldn't face that last moment of reality, the second of pain.

There was no distinction as to age or sex. If someone fell by the side of the road, the swift flash of a soldier's bayonet, perhaps with blood still dripping from it, would make that fall permanent.

Another father was also carrying his child and Chea

34

could see that the man's knees were getting wobbly. Suddenly he fell to the side of the road. In seconds a soldier moved over and with one quick thrust nailed the father and baby to the ground. Neither they nor the soldier made a sound. Chea jerked his head forward. The image of the little drowned girl melted into a montage with what he had just seen, but he quickly told himself, "There was nothing I could do." He kept walking.

Then Chea's clouded perception sensed a familiar sight. Only a short distance down the road was a small pine tree preserve. The road cut through the grove, giving it an idyllic setting. There he and Khom used to stop and eat lunch when they hiked up to where the stones were found. A small stream ran parallel to the road for a few yards. Perhaps, Chea hoped, they could make a rest stop there. It would be a chance to put their feet in the water, or at least to get out of the sun.

Khom saw the trees too and whispered to his father, "We are coming to our resting place."

"Maybe they'll let us stop and sit in the shade for a little while," said Chea.

"I would rather be a moving target than a sitting one," said Khom.

"No one has been killed for at least thirty minutes. Maybe they've killed everyone they're going to kill."

Their conversation was drowned out by a shrill scream from the front of the procession. The people in the middle and back picked up their pace to see what was happening.

Chea and his family had moved only a few yards when they could see the clearing to the side of the road. He gasped, then cursed, as he saw the tree that he and Khom used to sit under to eat lunch. From one of the branches hung a large body, naked and emasculated. There were bayonet holes all over the chest and abdomen. Chea vomited as he saw that the body was hanging by a bright blue silk scarf. The Colonel's children's army was strewn over the clearing, some stripped, all dead.

A cry of desperation rose above the sobbing. Chea recognized the voice, moving fast toward the clearing through the crowd and shouting, "My son, my son, my son!" A short burst of machine-gun fire told Chea that if he ever got back to his village, he would need a new clerk.

People began to fall to the ground. The guards did not move. Everyone sat in the road, staring at the horrendous scene before them. Disbelief struck Chea. These are our people. They can't kill their own people. They can't.

The foreboding that had haunted him for so many nights was replaced by deep darkness. As he sat on the road, a strange feeling began to invade his mind. "For eleven years I worked with Clerk but I never really knew him. I hardly knew he had a son, yet he must have loved him as much as I love Khom." Chea tried to shake off the feeling, but it clung to his mind. "Clerk was human. He was a real person, but to me he was a thing. Someone who would listen to my tales of hardship, although I never listened to his. He was little more than a tape recorder into which I fed my words. How many times could I have helped him? When his two children died, I gave him a little money—but was that what he really needed, or should I have done something more human?" The words that someone had given him, and he had placed under the glass of his desk, came to mind, adding despair to his darkness: "If you have done it to one of my children, you have done it unto me."

He wanted to run to Clerk and tell him he was sorry, but he knew it was too late. A time had passed and it would never return. "Maybe the guards will let me take Clerk and his son and bury them together. At least they deserve that much," Chea said half aloud.

The shout of the guards ended that idea. With their bayonets they were prodding people to their feet. Chea and his family slowly lifted themselves off the dirt road. The cloud of depression weighed on him, along with a terrible desire for a drink of water.

He attempted to speak to Khom but realized that his mouth was too dry to open. He worked up some saliva and with his tongue moistened his stuck-together lips. "There is water by the side of the road, remember?"

"Yes," replied Khom, who was also having trouble speaking.

"Let's gradually move over that way and, when we pass, you can reach down and quickly fill your hand."

The two moved closer to the side of the road, Chea still carrying Pha. After a few minutes they were by the side of the road. The water was near. Chea did not see anyone else bending over. That was good. The others would act as a shield. "The water is about here. Try to get some."

Still walking, Khom squatted and stuck his hand into the grass by the roadside. He brought it up empty.

"Well, try again after we walk a few more steps."

In a few moments he looked cautiously to both sides. No soldiers around. "Now!" he whispered to Khom.

Khom repeated his little genuflex. He brought his hand up, full of water. Both gasped and Khom quickly threw the water to the ground. His hand was still bright red. He wiped it off on his trousers. Now Chea knew why no one was trying to dip water from the roadside.

Mercifully, clouds began to cover the sun. Chea knew that the monsoon rains were near and it would probably rain in a couple of hours. He looked at Wife.

All color had drained from her face. Her back was arched from carrying Baby Sister. "Can she walk for awhile?" he asked.

"No," she croaked through her swollen lips. "I carried her for nine months, and I can carry her again, as far as they want to take us."

Her firmness was a tonic to Chea's sinking spirit. Maybe, he thought, he was wrong again. Maybe Wife was really the strength of the family. Perhaps only his vanity had kept him from admitting it. His depression began to deepen, but then was washed away as rain began to fall lightly. Puffs of dust rose from the road as it fell. In a few minutes it was as if he were standing under his shower. People turned their heads heavenward and opened their mouths while not daring to slacken their pace. In a few minutes water was on the road, and people stooped quickly to pick up handfuls where others had left footprints. Khom reached down and came up with part water and part mud. He placed it in Pha's mouth, with most of it running down Chea's back. Several times he repeated the process until Pha, Baby Sister, and his mother had at least their lips moistened. The cooling effect of the rain was as a "gift of great price" to the people. Before, they had looked at rain as something to run from. Now it was something to stand in, walk under, feel each drop as it hit one's head, washing away the heat of the sun and the dust of the road.

The rain continued, and so did the forced march. It was beginning to get dark. No one had had any food all day, and seemingly none would be available. Chea slackened his pace, beginning to think about where they were going and what they would do when they got there.

For the first time in seven hours Pha loosened her hold on her father's neck. Gently he asked her if she would like to walk on the cool ground for a little while. "It will refresh you," he said, "and you might enjoy it."

Without saying a word, Pha slid down, careful not to stumble. She moved up behind her mother and fell in step.

Chea was a few steps behind when he noticed that the footprints in the mud were red with blood. Wife had lost her sandals, and each time she took a step she left a bloody imprint. Quickly Chea walked up beside her. "When did you lose your sandals?" he asked sternly.

"Back when you stumbled."

"But that was hours ago. Why didn't you tell me?"

She did not respond. He moved a few feet in front of her and stepped out of his sandals. Without missing a motion she stepped into them, wincing as she took the first few steps. Chea could see the blood now forming on the extra space of the sandals. He looked down at her delicate swollen feet, and the black cloud of depression swooped down and engulfed him. Why hadn't he noticed earlier? "Surely," he murmured to no one in particular, "this many people should not have to suffer this much, just to open the eyes of one man." The thought caused him to shiver.

The rain stopped as quickly as it had started. The refreshing it brought caused Chea to think about food. His stomach ached.

Darkness comes quickly in Cambodia. One moment it is light, and the next moment you have to have a flashlight to avoid the snakes, scorpions, and other nocturnal creatures.

The front part of the ragged parade began to stop. Chea stood up on his toes to see what was happening. A soldier moved back shouting, "Sit! Sit!"

All of them sat right where they were. If they landed in a mud puddle, they stayed there.

Another soldier moved along giving orders. "This is

where you will spend the night. If anyone moves from the road, he will be shot." The soldiers moved over to the side of the road, while several stood guard.

Chea gathered his family around him and gently took Little Sister off Wife's back. For the first time since ten that morning, the burden of a two-year-old child was removed. Wife winced with pain, attempting to straighten up. Her face was gaunt and her eyes were beginning to swell. Her lips were nearly twice their normal size. "How beautiful she is," Chea thought. It was something he had hardly noticed in the previous thirteen years.

No one attempted to move about. People stretched out wherever they had landed. Chea took off his *sampot* and, sitting in his undershorts, laid it on the ground. He motioned his wife to lie on it. She did not argue. She lay stretched out on her back enjoying the dry warmth of the cloth. The wet muck soon soaked through, but she didn't seem to mind. She took Baby Sister and laid her on top of her, trying to give her some warmth. In moments, both were asleep.

The soldiers began cooking supper only a few yards away, and the smell was excruciating. Chea could see the flames from the small fire they had built. No noise rose from the camp, from either the hunters or their prey.

Chea stretched out on his side so that Khom and Pha could lean against him. Pha quickly went to sleep. Khom sat looking across to the campfire.

"I'm proud of you, son. You're a good soldier."

"Their day will come, and I hope I'm here when it does," Khom responded bitterly, ignoring his father's gentle remark.

His words cut into Chea's mind. All his life Chea had prided himself on being nonviolent. It was the way he had been reared, and he expected to bring up his children the same way. They were never allowed to discuss war around the table, or even in the house.

"The real victims of war are the survivors," he intoned whenever the subject was broached. The very tone of his voice signaled the end of the conversation, and Wife quickly changed the subject. Now he could see hatred burning in Khom's eyes. It was different from what he saw in the soldiers' eyes. Their eyes were empty. They were zombies, being kept around for awhile to carry out one more task for their master before they too would be destroyed. The look in his son's eyes was not death but revenge, a subject antithetical to Chea's entire life-style. Chea reached down gently and stroked mud out of Khom's hair. His son too was asleep.

Chea looked at the boy and was stricken with an overwhelming desire to take him to the mountains one more time. This time they would not learn how to get stones from the earth, or how to bargain with the hill people. He would spend those hours explaining other principles that would extinguish that flame of revenge.

Chea slipped into a fitful sleep, and then suddenly it was morning. He had slept straight through the quiet moments of the day, or did such a time no longer exist? Had it died at the end of a bayonet?

Soldiers were walking beside the group shouting at them. "Everyone on your feet. Move! Move!"

The agony of having to pry the children from their sleep made Chea feel as though he could never get out of the mud. He wanted to stay there and die.

Wife stood up and without a word took her sleeping baby and put her back in the saddle. Khom rose and shook his head. "I'm hungry," he said without thinking.

Chea got up slowly, lifting Pha with him. He was going to have to carry her. She was awake, but her body seemed unable to respond to the need to walk. Chea

41

bent over, picked up the mud-soaked *sampot* from the ground, and wrapped it around him.

As his little family began their new day of exodus, they watched the road, moving gently around people who were either dead or dying. They heard screams from behind them, but no one looked back. The soldiers were killing the sick and dying. The screams ended, and several soldiers returned to join the column. Chea looked back. Relief swept over him to see that Smiling One was not among them.

Several hours down the road, several *bonzes*, or priests, joined the group, along with two new soldiers who looked no different from the others. If Chea hadn't known the others by sight, he wouldn't have noticed the new arrivals. The *bonzes* had been stripped of their robes and beads and were wearing only undershorts. One, no more than twelve or thirteen years old, was burned raw by the sun. It was the custom for many children to spend time in the temple as novices. The other two were older, perhaps in their early thirties. All three died before the afternoon rains came.

The rains quit, and evening darkness started to fall. The group began to turn off the road. A soldier led them through the trees to a clearing about forty yards away. The soft dirt felt good. The grass between their toes was a refreshment they had taken for granted before.

The soldiers gave a signal for everyone to sit. Again the darkness approached so fast that in a few moments all was pitch blackness. Chea's family huddled together and one by one fell asleep. Chea could only hope that tomorrow would not bring another day of forced march. As the moon came out he could see the huddled mass of people, no more than three hundred still alive. Two days of marching, all those people murdered, and many more dying right now. Little wonder, he thought, that the moon is red tonight. He looked up at the stars and saw one moving across the sky. It was a satellite, and hope welled up in him. He had read that space satellites could pick up objects as small as the group he was in. Maybe the Americans were watching their progress, sending the news around the world. His journalist friends whom he had met at the border on his selling trips would take the story and send it to the far corners of the earth. He knew what the press could do with public opinion. Now, surely those same people would respond to the genocide being committed against their former Cambodian allies.

THREE

Chea awoke to the sound of a child moaning. Ignoring the pain that flamed throughout his body, he quickly sat up. He held his hands to his ears, straining to identify the sound. Hearing nothing, he shook his head and slowly lay back on the ground. Again he heard the soft moan.

He sat up and looked at his wife, her face pointing skyward, heavy sleep still compassionately holding her. Khom was lying with his head across Chea's legs, Pha on the other side. Little Sister was missing. Chea lay motionless, trying to quiet his pounding heart and straining for the sound once again. He heard it. He turned his head in the direction from which it came. He stared into the darkness but could see nothing.

Gently he slid one leg out from under Khom's head, easing the boy's head to the ground. He then repeated the process with Pha. He raised himself to his knees, then to his feet, and began to walk in a half-crouched position, moving cautiously in the direction from which he had heard the moan. He heard it again, a little to the right. He moved faster, still crouched down so as not to be silhouetted against the sky. He did not want the soldier on guard to think he was trying to escape. He moved quietly, stopping abruptly as he came upon another sleeping family.

He again heard the sound a little farther away. Crawling toward it, he pleaded for strength, for wisdom, for anything that would get him to Baby Sister before they discovered her. Day came as quickly as night, and dawn, just beginning to break, would soon light up the landscape. There would be no hiding then.

He stopped and whispered, "Baby Sister, Baby Sister, where are you?" No reply. He kept moving in the same direction. Suddenly he froze and slid to his knees. A few yards away Chea could see the outline of a soldier with his gun by his side. Perhaps he was sleeping, perhaps on guard. He slid back and started to circle around him.

The cry came again, and this time he knew it was his daughter. Forgetting the soldier, he started crawling in the direction of the sound. His eyes burned as he stared into the grey dawn. His heart seemed about to pound its way out of his chest.

Then he saw her. The little silhouette of Baby Sister walking around the camp. He crawled faster, but she kept moving. She stumbled over sleeping forms and fell. Getting up again, she turned in his direction. Soon they were within a few feet of each other. If he spoke to her, she might cry out to him. She turned again and started in the opposite direction. Quickly he crawled up behind her, and with one movement, he grabbed her, putting his hand over her mouth. He held her close to him, and whispered in her ear, "It's all right, Penh. Daddy's home."

The little girl relaxed in his arms. "Daddy, I'm sick."

"Come, I'll take you back to Mommy."

"No, I want to go back home. I'm sick. Please, Daddy, we play this game long time. Please, let's go home. I want some food. I want my dolly. Please, Daddy."

For the first time, Baby Sister began to cry. Chea lay on the ground and held her close as she wept into his shoulder. After several minutes people began to stir, and before he could return to his family a soldier walked about, kicking people, yelling at them to get up.

Chea wasn't sure where his family was. Crawling around in the dark, he had become disoriented. As people began to stand up, he stood and then began to retrace what he thought were his steps.

In a few minutes he came upon three people huddled together on the ground. "What's the matter?" he asked.

Wife looked up, and began to cry.

Khom looked at him and with fear in his voice said, "We thought you had taken Little Sister and escaped."

The very idea that he might do such a thing, the accusation from his son, caused Chea to feel weak. He sat down, still holding Little Sister. He could only look at his family, speechless, as they stared at him. All the life seemed to have gone out of Pha. Khom continued looking at his father with skepticism. Chea tried to explain. "I woke up, and she was gone. I went looking for her."

"We knew better," said Wife. "We knew you wouldn't leave us." She looked at him, her eyes asking forgiveness. One glance told her she was forgiven. Khom turned and faced the other direction.

Chea grieved. The family circle of trust had been broken. He had to mend it, but he didn't know how. He wasn't sure even where to start. He got up and put his hand on Khom's shoulder. "Come, we better get ready in case we have to move."

Actually, there was nothing to get ready. They were wearing everything they owned. It was only something to mollify the hurt and distrust that were in the air.

Everyone sat quietly in family groups for several

hours. There was still no food. With an empty stomach, the body fed on itself, creating dehydration, nausea, numbness. Those who were under bushes and trees escaped the morning sun. Others had to remain totally exposed, even though it was common for the temperature to rise to 110 degrees before the afternoon rain cooled things off.

Chea heard people talking about how kind the guards were to let them rest for a change. He felt the same way. "Funny," he thought. "Here are men who have killed, murdered over two hundred of our villagers, and now we are paying them tribute for their kindness."

The sound of an approaching vehicle could be heard making its way to the clearing. Chea saw that it was the type of vehicle that the daily messenger had used in the village. When it was close, it drew to a stop. Several soldiers went up to it and stood without speaking to its occupant. The Stranger who had made the speech in the village square got out on the passenger's side. He walked toward the villagers with slow, short steps, surveying them.

Then he motioned the huddled group of refugees forward, just as he had done to the family in the village square. Several soldiers stood on each side of him. Fear spread through the crowd. Some turned and looked in the direction of the forest. Three soldiers stood between them and the trees, their rifles no longer cradled in their arms. There was no escape. The villagers rose and reluctantly moved toward the Stranger. Some stayed on their knees; they wouldn't have so far to fall in death. No one wanted to be in front.

Chea took his entire family and tried to put his arm around them. They were near the front. He tried to let others past, but Khom insisted on moving to the front. There would be no chance for survival.

Chea whispered to Wife, "If they start shooting, fall

on the children, and I'll fall on you. Pretend you're dead, and don't move."

Khom heard him and looked back; he registered no fear. Pha lost the ability to use her legs, so Chea picked her up and carried her. The Stranger lifted his hands to indicate they had come close enough. He turned to the soldiers standing beside him and nodded.

The soldiers put down their rifles and walked back to the truck. Chea felt gratitude to the Stranger welling up inside of him. It was a feeling he hated, but it was spontaneous. Others showed their gratitude by standing up and smiling, releasing their grip on each other. Khom looked disappointed as he continued to grit his teeth.

The Stranger began to speak. This time he did not need a public address system. His audience was only a fraction of what it had been three days earlier. Only the healthy remained.

"Welcome to your new home." He half smiled as he spoke. "It is time for everyone to use their hands to build a new Kampuchea. While we have been out fighting all these years, you have been eating too much food and getting fat. Well, now you are going to be the ones to feed us." He liked that line and repeated it, then went on. "Everyone needs hard physical labor. If you don't work, you won't eat. This piece of ground is to be cleared."

He swept his hand around, indicating the piece of land that ran into the forest on both sides and up against a hill on the other, but not more than a quarter of a square mile in size. It was covered with elephant grass, weeds, rocks, and trees. "The Supervisor here will remain with you today and get you started." He pointed to a skinny, obsequious little man standing by the truck.

Without another word the Stranger crawled into the truck and slammed the door. The driver gunned the motor and began to turn around. "We will bring you food tonight," the Stranger yelled.

The feeling of gratitude returned, if only for a second.

The Supervisor, wearing the same kind of khaki uniform with a straw helmet, stepped forward. His voice was high pitched and nervous. "All men above the age of twelve are to report to me. Women and children, stay where you are."

Most of the fathers had survived the death march, so over half of the remaining people came forward. They were told to sit on the ground in groups. The Supervisor began to point. "This group here will be unit one; this group, unit two; this one, unit three; this one, unit four. Do not forget your unit number. You will live with your unit. There will be no unnecessary talking. All men and boys will clear the fields. All women who can walk will go to the edge of the forest and gather berries, roots, and greens for your food. The old ones will take care of the babies."

He stopped moving back and forth and looked at them with piercing eyes. "If any woman does not come back from the work detail, her entire family will be executed. Publicly! If any man tries to escape, his entire unit will be executed. Understood? You will rise at 5:30, and head for your work at six. You will return to your homes at eleven o'clock and eat your first meal. There will be no eating in the mornings; we must conserve food. We will quit working at 7:00 P.M., and you will have one hour to eat the meal prepared by the children and old women. After the meal we will have re-education meetings. Now, unit one, over there; unit two, over here."

One by one he pointed out where each unit was to set up headquarters. "Today the women will pull down palm leaves for your shelter. You men will start clearing the ground for your new homes." With that, he turned and walked away as the men headed for their unit areas.

Chea moved to the area designated as unit three. His family followed him. Together they stood and looked around them. They were surrounded by grass, dirt, and rocks, but without so much as a fingernail file to use as a tool.

Soon seven other families joined the group. Chea knew some by name, others by sight. Several were strangers to him. One, whom Chea knew, suggested that the men elect a unit leader. In a few minutes they had elected Chea. Khom started to object, but a glance from his father silenced him.

They agreed that each family would remain together. Chea instructed the women to go to the edge of the forest and look for fronds to build shelters. He was careful to remind them that their families would be executed if they didn't come back.

Wife took Pha's hand and began to walk toward a grove of trees where other women were also heading. Her daughter leaned on her as she walked.

Sitting on the ground, Baby Sister asked, "Daddy, when we have breakfast?"

"Later," he told her.

The men started pulling weeds, and Khom carried some of the larger stones to the area marking their territory.

After several hours the women returned. They carried branches and palm fronds they had broken off the trees. They piled them in the small area that the men had cleared of as much grass as possible.

As the women fell to the ground exhausted, some crying, some cursing, the men began sorting through the branches, distributing them so that each family could start at once to build a lean-to as protection from sun and rain.

A short time later Chea stood back and looked at the

palm fronds leaning precariously against four sticks he had broken off the branches. He didn't know how long it would stand, but it was a shelter.

Wife looked at it with approval and then at Pha, who was leaning listlessly against her. The child's lips were badly swollen and cracked in several places. Raw flesh made up a large part of her bottom lip. Her face was white, a wrenching contrast to the dark black circles under her puffy eyes.

Chea was laying her under the shelter when a truck moved into the clearing. "That must be our food," he thought, feeling her hot forehead. Then he began to walk toward the truck.

The idea that there would be food gave the villagers a momentary injection of energy as they moved toward where the vehicle was coming to a stop. A soldier in the back of the truck got up. He threw a box of empty condensed milk cans on the ground and jumped down. His rifle never left his hands.

The Supervisor, who had moved behind a clump of bushes after his speech earlier that day, reappeared. He walked over to the cans and picked one up. The top of the can had been removed, making it into a cup without a handle.

"These are your eating utensils. There are not enough for one for each person, so we will give a couple to each unit." He then motioned as he spoke. "Come, get your cups."

Each unit leader went forward and picked up several cups. Chea was the last one. Four cans remained. He picked them up and returned to his place. He could feel tension building up. The villagers could see no food. Not many could last another night without some kind of nourishment.

A soldier jumped back into the truck and pulled out a couple of bolts. The side of the truck came down, exposing several bags of rice.

With the rest, Chea let out an audible moan. Hunger pangs took hold of his stomach. He moved his fist down and held it against the empty, burning pit.

The soldier pulled a knife from a sheath at his side and cut open one of the bags. The Supervisor strolled over and took a milk can from a man in the front row. He walked back, stood by the truck, and held up the cup. "This holds 250 grams of rice. You will each receive one cup."

The agony of hunger clashed with the fear of being first to step forward. A nod from the Supervisor and you would never need rice again. Haggard, wasted, sunburned, the villagers waited for a cue that would give them a new lease on life.

The Supervisor broke the silence. "Unit leaders, come forward and get your rice. Bring something to put it in."

The villagers looked at their cups, at each other, and then one man tore off his dirty shirt and laid it at the Supervisor's feet. The Supervisor took the cup and measured, counting out eighteen cans of rice. Then with his foot he pointed to the shirt with the small stack of food, motioning him to take it. Another stepped forward, and then another.

When Chea's turn came, he stepped forward and took off his shirt. He tied a knot in the back where it had been torn, and laid it at the Supervisor's feet.

"You will get twenty-two cans of rice," the Supervisor said with a knowing smile.

How did he know there were twenty-two people in Chea's unit? Then, as the Supervisor carefully counted out the twenty-two cans of rice, Chea realized that not much would happen in this camp that the little man who lived behind the bush didn't know.

When the last unit leader had his rice, the soldier lifted up the side of the truck and jumped in. Chea noticed three more boxes in the back. In one, at least, were more milk cans. Chea's heart ached as the truck pulled away. For the first time he realized that out in the darkness that was now descending there were other camps like this one, other Khmer people whose hearts ached, whose children were dying, whose wives' feet were bleeding. Sick and desperately sad, he slowly walked back to his unit with the rice. His hunger pains had been replaced by a greater pain for his people. Sadness he couldn't give words to hung over him as he stood beside the dejected villagers from his unit.

When he put down the rice, the twenty-one other people began to talk excitedly, all at the same time.

"What are we supposed to cook with?"

"Rice, but no way to cook it."

"Water—we have no water."

"Yes, there is a stream down there, not far."

A woman spoke up. "Others will have to go; we will follow them."

"Come, give me your cans and we will fill them."

Before half an hour had passed, women who were used to baked-clay ovens, cooking pots, jugs, bowls, rice ladles, water pitchers, and colorful serving mats, now squatted over little fires with a few used milk cans half full of rice and water.

Chea removed his can from the fire, and with sticky fingers carefully took some of the half-boiled rice and put it between Little Sister's lips. She ate it quickly and asked for more. He kept scooping out of the milk can, and soon it was empty. Only then did he realize that no rice was left on his shirt to cook. It all had been eaten, and Chea was still without food. As Little Sister began chattering about the nice house they had, and how good the rice was, and the other things that excited her, Chea leaned back to rest. Pha moved from her mother's lap and regurgitated her rice on the ground.

Chea ate for the first time in four days.

FOUR

Chea's ability to withstand affliction grew, along with the calluses on his hands and feet. He made a calendar by placing small stones on a dried leaf, one stone for every day, one piece of wood for each month. Three pieces of wood and four stones lay in the corner of the small hut that had replaced the lean-to. Here the family rested for an hour in the afternoon, and slept at night, when sickness and bugs permitted it. Just outside was a small circle of rocks, where all the food was cooked. The milk cans had been replaced with cans one size larger. Now enough food could be cooked for two people at a time, and it took only half as long to prepare a meal. Each family lived as a unit and handled its own food. No social intercourse was allowed. Each day the women gathered leaves, roots, and berries which were then mixed with the rice. No one had time to boil the water, and dysentery plagued the camp.

Baby Sister returned to her usual good humor, while the rest of the family made a project out of disguising reality for her. Because she was shielded from the tragedies that struck any time of the day or night, she continued to sparkle like a jewel in a dung heap.

Though Chea's wife regained some of her strength, like everyone else, she grew a little weaker each day. The 250 grams of rice, without any meat, was below subsistence level, especially since they were working so hard.

Some lived better than others for awhile. Two cans of rice were sold for a small bag of gold. Four tangerines brought by the Supervisor were sold for an "offering" of nineteen watches that suddenly appeared from men's *sampots* or G-strings. Then the gold and watches were gone, and day-to-day survival equalized the villagers.

Khom had quizzed his father on three occasions about when they would escape. Each time his father rebuked him, reminding him that, if they escaped, the others in the unit would be killed.

One evening a mother didn't return from working on the edge of the forest. The Supervisor went looking for her. When he returned a short time later, the entire village watched as the missing woman's husband, two small children, and mother-in-law were led into the forest. There were no sounds. The soldiers returned in a few minutes; the family did not.

Since then, Khom hadn't brought the subject up, but the father-son relationship was strained. The suffering in Chea's heart was worse than having the hot sun beating down on him each day as he bent over his short-handled hoe, clearing the land. Their relationship had almost shattered three days earlier when Chea noticed that Khom, who often slept outside, had sneaked over to another unit. That was a violation of the Supervisor's orders, and if he were caught, he could be clubbed to death on the spot.

Chea pretended to be asleep when he heard Khom crawling back toward the hut. Later, he looked through the small opening and saw his son lying on his back, sound asleep. Around his neck, instead of his ivory dove, hung a grotesque amulet made from bark and berries. He could have gotten it only from the witch doctor who lived in another unit. Chea couldn't look at the grotesque figure. He decided to snatch it off his son, but as he reached for it Khom rolled over on his stomach.

The landscape changed little by little over the weeks as villagers continued to work and to die. The men had cleared a small area with their shortened hoes. The soldiers had broken off all but six inches of the hoe handles to use for their own purposes. The sound of AK-17s was replaced by the thud of hardwood hoe handles smashing a skull or breaking a neck. They were running short of ammunition, but not of targets.

To the right of the clearing were short, narrow mounds of leaves about the size of a person's body. That area grew larger each day. No one could afford to waste energy digging a very deep grave. The boys Khom's age were given hoes and a shovel, and each day they spent several hours digging holes of various lengths, two or three feet deep. A body was placed in the hole and covered with dirt and leaves. If there were two people to be buried and only one hole, one was placed on top of the other. Only workers and mourners went near the place, but often at noon, before the afternoon rain, the wind blew over the top of the mounds and the smell of death pervaded the camp.

The people worked from early morning till late at night. After the evening can of rice and leaves, the Supervisor would bring them together for a re-education meeting. The first night he harangued them for two hours. No one knew what he said, and Chea doubted that the Supervisor himself knew. Soldiers stood by, holding their hoe handles. No one dared sleep while the verbal assault continued. To make sure everyone was awake, they would often have them stand and sing the new song of the revolution:

CHAPTER FOUR

Red blood soaked the Cambodian Plain
Under the Revolution banner on the 17th
  of April
The blood dissolved the body of slavery.

Children under twelve were the only ones who didn't attend. Even the sick were carried out of their huts to listen and participate.

The Supervisor's squeaky voice seemed incongruous with what he had to say. It was obvious he knew little of Marxist ideology, though he took pride in calling himself a "full-fledged Khmer Rouge Marxist, following the great thinking of Mao Tse-tung."

He was eager that everyone understand he was no capitalist deviationist. Chea doubted he even knew what that meant, but he realized that the little man had to do something behind those bushes each day besides spy on the camp. "So," Chea told himself, "he probably writes speeches."

As Chea listened he began to realize that the Khmer Rouge's main interest wasn't in raising food. Any Khmer knew that with a little organization the fertile land of the Tongle Sap could supply not only their own country, but several other countries as well, with an abundance of rice—as it had been doing before. Chea began to suspect that because these people couldn't administer cities, they simply moved everyone to the countryside. "What better way," thought Chea, "to get rid of what they called their 'dead weight,' which included school teachers, regular government soldiers, religious leaders, and anyone who had more than a third-grade education." No one had used a moving graveyard before. He wondered if that was planned or if it just happened.

Evidently the speeches soon bored the Supervisor as well as the villagers. Fewer and fewer re-education meetings were called. When they had meetings, they consisted more of harangues to work harder and produce more, than of ideological diatribes. The only other diversion in the camp was the gossip circuit. One rumor fed on another, lifting hopes or spreading despair, depending on the words passed. Walking in the field, one person would whisper to another:

"American soldiers are on their way."

"The world press is putting so much pressure on the Khmer Rouge that we will soon be freed."

"Prince Sihanouk is back in Phnom Penh. When he finds out what is happening, he will set us free."

"Lon Nol's entire army has been executed, along with his cabinet."

"Murder is routine. Genocide is a possibility."

Chea was sure of only one thing. In the camp, rumors became fact, gossip became reality.

Chea bent over his hoe, digging out some stubborn roots from a plant. While working he always kept thinking. They could kill his body, but not his spirit. "That does not belong to them and they cannot touch it," he would remind his hoe. "They can beat me senseless with their little hoe handles, or fill me full of the contents of a dozen 'banana clips' from their AK-17s, but they can not touch my spirit," he would remind himself as he drove the hoe into the root. It was his only comfort in a comfortless world. Another workday ended on signal, and Chea straightened his back and began to trudge back to the hut.

On the way he passed several of the soldiers who walked through the camp making sure that the sick were really sick, that everyone was in the right unit, that no one was talking or making weapons. As he approached his hut, he saw a soldier standing nearby, holding his hoe handle. Chea quickened his pace toward home. The soldier saw him coming and moved off. It was his former Sunday school student, Smiling One. Still no recognition, though Chea was positive that the soldier knew who he was.

As Chea approached his hut he saw Wife leaning over Pha. Khom was standing to the side. Baby Sister was building a little house out of sticks. Pha lay on the ground, her eyes closed, lips parched.

"I think it's malaria," said his wife.

He knelt beside Pha. His hand moved across her brow. He could feel the heat, but there was no sweat. She was too dehydrated to perspire.

Chea looked up at Khom, who had turned his back. He ordered his son to hurry and get a can of water.

Without looking at his father, Khom reached down, picked up a can, and went for the only medicine in the camp, dirty water from a stagnant pool.

Throughout the evening Chea wiped Pha's forehead with his dampened shirt. He just had to believe that she would run again and smile and shop in the market with her mother, sing and play the guitar with her friends at church, and one day receive from someone a white scarf to "fix the words and tie the heart."

The quiet of his thoughts was broken by a thud on the side of the hut. Everyone was startled except Pha, who was moaning in delirium.

Khom reached over and picked up a leaf tightly wrapped with a blade of grass. Chea grabbed it from him and tore it open. Hope spread across his face. "Look," he said, holding out six quinine tablets.

"Who threw them?" asked Wife.

"I don't know," said Chea, "but do you know what this means?" He bent down and whispered to Pha. "We have some quinine, little daughter. You're going to get well." He took a can of water, held her head up with one hand, and put a quinine tablet in her mouth. He gave her a little water, closed her mouth, and laid her back down. He then leaned over, rubbed his nose on her cheek, and blew loudly. It was the last time he kissed her.

When morning light began to streak across the camp, Chea picked up Pha. His wife lifted her arms over his shoulders. Chea, Wife, and Khom headed for the edge of camp.

Yesterday Khom had dug several shallow places. Now the grieving entourage headed in that direction to fill one of those small holes with dirt, leaves, and precious little Pha.

FIVE

The death of Pha changed Chea's life in several ways.
The unshed tears of Wife seemed to dig a deep chasm
between them. He could reach across and touch her,
but she was a dead person on furlough. Chea's heart
burned with new desire to comfort her, but she
remained apart from all around her. A part of her had
died, and she hadn't found anything to replace it.

Like an automaton, she would cook, bow her head,
eat, wash clothes, admonish Baby Sister in a monotone, go to the forest, gather food, and return.

In addition to that new burden, which in past times
would have in itself been enough to crush his spirit,
Chea had the ominous feeling that the last strand
binding father and son had snapped. Khom now
blatantly displayed the amulet he had gotten from the
kru, making sure that his father saw him holding it at
meal times while the rest bowed their heads.

Still unaffected was Baby Sister, whose only question was "When big sister come home from school?"
She continued to build stick houses, make stick dolls,
and smile at anyone who crossed in front of the hut.
Only once did Chea have to admonish her. Arriving

back from the clearing, he caught her entertaining children from another unit by making a speech in which she not only sounded but looked very much like the Supervisor. At any other time or place it would have caused much merriment, but now things were different. Such an act was enough to warrant a hoe handle across her head with enough force to break open her skull.

Chea himself missed his oldest daughter more than he could verbalize. Even now, as he bent over his hoe, digging a straight line in which to plant the seeds, he was rehearsing what he liked best about her. The thoughts of her being gone was too much to add to his aching muscles, burning back, and grief over Wife and Khom.

He was suddenly brought back to reality by the shout of "Freeze!" It was one of the Supervisor's ways of instilling discipline. Any time, day or night, he would sneak into the camp and yell just that one word. All in hearing distance were to freeze in whatever position they were. To move was to get a hoe handle across your back. Sometimes the people stood frozen over boiling cans of rice until the fire went out and the rice got cold. Other times it would be only seconds before he yelled, "Work!" and everyone could continue their activity.

The men stood still in various poses. Chea had just dug his hoe into the ground, all ready to pull it up, when he heard the command. He leaned against what remained of the handle, making the process less excruciating. The mid-morning sun beat down on their backs. Someone moved, and Chea heard the thud of a hoe handle hitting flesh, breaking it open for the sun to sear.

Chea often counted time in large sections: morning, noon, afternoon, evening. It was the way camp life was broken up. Now he counted it in seconds. There were short seconds and long seconds. The sweat ran down his back and he tried to imagine sweat beads having a race to get off his back. He counted the weeds just below his eyes, wishing he could change places with them. He leaned a little on his hoe, but could feel it slide. If he leaned too much, he would slip, and then the hoe handle in the hands of a soldier would slam across his back.

His feet began to burn: first his toes and then just below his ankles. His thongs hadn't survived the long march. He felt as if he were standing in hot water that was being brought to a boiling point. He moved his eyes, looked down, and involuntarily gasped as he saw what was happening. He was standing in the middle of an anthill. Slowly the red ants were eating their way across his feet and up his ankles. He had seen what they could do to a dead boar in the mountains with their voracious appetite; they could strip the flesh off a bone and leave it white as bleached limestone.

Should he move and risk being killed by a soldier's hoe handle, or should he allow himself to be eaten alive? Did he want to die quickly or slowly? He watched incredulously as more and more of the tiny monsters made their way over his toes and up his ankle. It had started with just one ant, but that one had given the signal. Food! Now it had been joined by thousands of others. Chea couldn't hold on much longer. He was soon going to have to choose whether he wanted to die screaming, or with a sudden blow. The ants moved past his ankle onto his right leg. He lost all sense of time as he watched them moving like a red sock being pulled up over his foot. He made his decision. I will count to ten, scream, and fall—scraping the ants off as I do. They kept moving up his leg. For some reason there were only a few on his left leg, and even those now seemed to be moving onto the right one. He closed his eyes. He had made his decision. He opened his mouth to scream, to let out all the frustrations he had felt in the past months—at "them," his son, his daughter, his wife, the world. He opened his mouth and then heard the Supervisor's words, "Back to work."

He fell to the ground and, using both hands, started scraping off the ants. He rubbed dirt on his leg, hoping to kill more of the little cannibals. Reaching for a second handful, he noticed that his hands were red with blood. The mud around his leg was soaked with blood. He took his hoe handle and began to scrape his leg, removing the dirt and most of the ants. When a soldier yelled "Go home," he picked off the remaining few ants and tried to stand. He looked with disbelief at his foot, a raw mass of flesh from the toes up halfway to the knee. He moved his other foot as he felt a sting and realized he had again stood in the anthill. He quickly scraped off the new invaders and began to limp toward his hut, eyes half closed, teeth clenched in pain.

He fell down in front of the fire where an old woman was preparing rice and greens. Wife hadn't yet arrived from her working area. Khom took one look at his father's legs and went behind the hut. Chea could hear him vomit.

It took five days for the burning to subside. The wound was grotesque. Khom would take his food and eat behind the hut to avoid seeing it. Wife would pour warm water over the raw flesh, but only Baby Sister showed sympathy. She would stand beside him, patting his knee. "Feel better soon. Feel better soon. Don't cry, Daddy."

He didn't cry, at least not visibly, as the foot turned into a running sore. There was neither medicine nor excuse for missing work. Each day he would go to the clearing, dig furrows, go home, eat, rest, and go back to the field. After another week, the swelling went down, and his right leg was only about a third again as big as his left. The seed had finally arrived, and they could start putting something into the furrows they had dug, covered up, and re-dug.

Early one afternoon the truck delivered three bags of corn. Each man had to bring an empty milk can, fill it with corn, and then move down the row placing seeds an inch apart and covering up the row as he went.

To place raw corn into the hands of starving men caused new problems. Chea wrestled with the idea for most of the morning. Would eating it be stealing? He had never stolen in his life. Should he start now? When the guard turned and walked in the opposite direction, Chea flipped a kernel into his mouth. He chewed on it carefully. It didn't have much taste, but Chea knew it would give him strength. Before the afternoon was over he had devised a plan. Every third seed he would place on his thumb and flick up into his mouth quicker than a soldier could blink. The idea that his stomach had something in it made him feel stronger.

It took them four days to plant the corn. They were finishing the last row when he looked up and saw the Supervisor with two guards standing beside him.

He was sure he had been caught. Yet he hadn't put any in his mouth for most of the row. His conscience was controlled by his stomach, and he never ate as much corn after lunch as before. It seemed less wrong just before a meal than after.

Clouds were covering the sun, but Chea was still sweating. The Supervisor walked over to another of the planters and stared, and then to another. Each man was responsible for one of the twenty-one rows.

The voice of the Supervisor cut through the mid-morning air. "I want everyone here," he said, pointing to the area in front of him. Soldiers passed the word to the women working at the far corner of the clearing and to the young boys at the graveyard. Old women and men began moving as fast as their emaciated bodies permitted.

Saying nothing, the Supervisor stood and watched. In a few minutes the one hundred eighty survivors stood at one end of the cornfield. Each of the twenty men stood by the row he had planted.

The Supervisor walked over to one side, bent over, and dug into the dirt covering the row. The villagers stared at him, motionless. He took a piece of corn out of the row, replaced the seed, and covered it. He moved on to the next row, repeating the process. At the sixth row he found no corn. He dug a little more. Still no corn. He went up to the villager, glared into his face, yelled "Parasite!" and kicked him in the groin. The man fell to the ground, doubled up with pain. The women moaned. The Supervisor ordered the soldiers to take the man over to a tree while he continued checking the rows. Chea's row was number thirteen. Ten, corn. Eleven, no corn. Another beating, another man taken to the tree at the end of the planting area. Twelve, corn. He walked up to Chea's row, this time starting in the middle. He bent on one knee, removed some dirt, found nothing, and dug around a little more. He held up a piece of corn, and then placed it back into the row, gently covering it. He moved farther down the row, repeating the process. The agony of waiting and guilt were building up inside Chea. He wanted to scream "Yes, I ate it, I ate it all. You were starving us to death. This corn will only rot anyway, with the monsoons. It's the wrong time of year to plant corn." The Supervisor held up another piece of corn, put it back in the ground, and covered it.

Row thirteen, corn. Row fourteen, corn. Row fifteen, no corn. The beating and the hauling away were repeated. Sixteen, seventeen through twenty-one, corn.

Clouds began to gather for the afternoon rain. The

Supervisor went over to the three men who had been thrown down by the soldiers at the bottom of the tree. He gave an order and a soldier ran to the truck, coming back with several pieces of wire used to tie rice sacks. The Supervisor ordered the three men to stand with their backs to the trees. Then the soldiers took their arms and wired them together so that they encircled the tree.

As they stood there, one yelled "Kill me, get it over with, kill me! You're going to kill us all anyway!"

The Supervisor looked at him and motioned for a soldier to put down his club. He spoke a few words to the soldiers and they walked a few yards to pick up the sacks of corn. They dumped the corn onto the ground and took the empty plastic bags over to the Supervisor.

Cries could be heard from the villagers, especially from the three men's relatives. The Supervisor placed the plastic bags over their heads, then tore off their clothing, and shredded it. From it, he made thin little ropes. One of the men was shouting from inside the bag. Another was trying to chew through his, but it kept sliding around. Soldiers braced their clubs against the men's legs so that they couldn't kick. With no more emotion than one would show if putting a rope around the neck of a water buffalo, the Supervisor wrapped a piece of cloth around each of the men's necks. Then, slowly, he went to each one and tightened it until no more air could get through, although not tight enough to choke the man. The Supervisor stood back to admire his work.

The sound of one of the men screaming under his plastic cover was drowned out by the wailing of his relatives. To Chea's astonishment, he himself never moved. He made no effort to help. He wasn't going to die trying to save three men.

The three were quickly using up the air in their plastic bags. One went limp and slid down the tree, dragging the other two with him. The harder the others fought, the tighter the wire got around their wrists. Because of the condensation, Chea could no longer see their faces inside the bags. The second man was sucking on his bag, and it looked like a hideous death mask outlining the form of his mouth and nose. The third man was taking deep breaths, quietly ending it as quickly as possible. In a few minutes it was all over. Another rumor had come true. Three more men were dead. A new precedent had been set in barbarity.

The Supervisor yelled, "Go home! Don't touch the bodies!" Weeping wives and mothers made their way to their huts. Chea turned and with a great tiredness began moving his legs, now sure of one thing. He must get help, he must escape. The man now dead had left an epitaph: "You're going to kill us all anyway." He couldn't bring those men back to life, any more than he could resurrect his daughter. But something had to be done. Someone had to stop these madmen before they destroyed the Khmer nation. Chea knew he must be that someone.

SIX

What corn hadn't been eaten had been planted. There was another piece of land to clear, and the men had been moved there. It was on the other side of the camp, beyond the tree where the three bodies still lay tied together, putrifying in the morning sun, soaking in the afternoon rain. Their smell joined the stench from the graveyard and the entire camp reeked of death.

Chea was certain he couldn't take any more nights of listening to children cry for food and sick people ask for medicine. He could not endure seeing the corpses waiting to be covered with a few leaves. Quiet, conservative, nonviolent Chea Aim was determining to get out of the camp and bring back the help he was sure was in Thailand. When the free world heard his story, tanks, guns, planes, but most of all the public opinion stirred up by journalists would end this terrible massacre. He no longer cared what would happen to the soldiers, the Supervisor, or even himself. He knew only that he had to bring help, not only to this camp but to the others as well that evidently were spread throughout the countryside.

After four hours of pulling branches, cutting vines,

and chopping ground, he still hadn't devised a plan. There seemed to be no options. If he made it into the woods and didn't come back, Khom, Wife, and Baby Sister would die. His family line would end in a pool of blood in an unmarked clearing. He could not entertain such an idea. As the work-day ended, he was out of ideas.

He made his way back to his family and a bowl of rice and weeds. No new thoughts came to him on how to help in some way more tangible than a bowed head and a recalled Bible verse.

The soldiers were making their rounds through the camp, checking to see that all the women had returned from the forest. As Chea turned to walk to his hut, he felt a heavy blow to his back. He fell forward and rolled over on his side, looking up. The Smiling One, the young soldier who once had sat so obediently in Chea's Sunday school classes reciting Bible verses and singing "Jesus loves me, this I know," now thrust his knee into Chea's stomach, holding him to the ground.

People nearby pretended they didn't see what was happening. Wife looked on from a distance, then she grabbed Baby Sister and disappeared into the hut.

Smiling One put a hand on each end of his hoe handle and brought it down across Chea's throat, showing no sign of emotion. He pushed on the club until Chea could barely breathe. Wife moaned like a wounded animal. Then the Smiling One spoke, low, and in gutteral tones. Chea was sure they were the last words he would ever hear.

"You must leave. They are going to send the women and children away from here. They will kill all the men. You must get help. Soon." Driving his knee into Chea's stomach even harder, he gave instructions. "Tomorrow, I will get you a map. I know a route." With each word he pressed down on the club for effect in case another soldier was watching. "I will wrap it in a leaf and throw it against your house. Listen for it."

One final thrust against Chea's throat and he passed out. Wife was pouring water on his face. Smiling One was nowhere around. Chea rubbed his bruised neck and tried to get up. His stomach revolted, and he sat back down. It wasn't a dream. He had the bruises to prove it. Wife helped him get to the hut, and he crawled inside. Baby Sister shouted, "Daddy's home," and he lay down on the mat, too sick to eat supper—or too excited. He couldn't share his secret with anyone. All night he lay there fighting sleep, waiting to hear for the second time the thud of a leaf-wrapped package hitting the side of his hut.

Morning came and he crawled outside, his stomach still aching and his neck black and blue. It was still hard to talk, and it hurt to swallow even water. He looked around outside the hut. Maybe he had gone to sleep without knowing it. There was no sign of a wrapped leaf.

Usually when Chea came outside, Khom would sit up, say nothing, and stroke his amulet—a gesture that Chea was certain was for his benefit and not because of any belief in the amulet's magic power. Then Khom would go off to work. This morning he just lay there.

Chea moved next to him and knelt down. Even before he touched him, he could feel heat coming from his body. "Malaria," he thought. Then, angrily, "You're sick. How long have you been sick? Why didn't you call me?"

His questions brought no response. Chea disappeared inside the hut and brought back the leaf with the quinine tablets. There were still five left. He took some water and made Khom take two of them. Khom didn't object.

Chea pulled Khom into the hut, making Baby Sister move over. Wife looked at the boy and immediately, without any sign of emotion, rose from the floor and

71

left the hut. When Chea came outside, she was standing looking into the distance.

"I've given him two quinine," whispered Chea. "He'll be all right now."

A workman appeared and told Chea that Khom had the only shovel. The soldier had given it to him to take care of. They needed it at the graveyard. Chea informed the young man that his son was sick with malaria and wouldn't be able to work today. The soldiers could come and check if they liked. They would see how sick he really was. The worker accepted his explanation and walked off toward the graveyard without the shovel.

Just as he was ready to leave for the field, Chea noticed the shovel leaning against the back of the hut. He picked it up, put it over his shoulders so that the soldiers could see what he was carrying, and headed for the graveyard. He would deliver the shovel and then report to his own work area.

He hadn't been to the graves since that morning they buried Pha. Now, so many graves had been added that he couldn't tell where hers was. It was one last indignity.

He spotted the man who had come for the shovel and took it over to him. He was standing beside a grave. Just as Chea turned to leave, two soldiers approached from behind the bushes. One was carrying the shoulders, the other the feet of a young soldier, one of their own. They came up to the grave and threw down the lifeless body. "Here, bury this one too," they said as they walked away laughing.

Chea looked down and saw a note pinned to the young soldier's shirt: "He was not one of us." In spite of the bruises on his face he had a peaceful look. Chea knew now there would be no map and no escape. Smiling One was dead.

SEVEN

Chea set down his hoe. Another day was over, and he had been given a new lease on life. He had a plan for escape. He had cleared more land than three other men while devising it, but he was sure it was inspired. His only problem was that it would take the cooperation of both Wife and sullen, sick Khom. They not only had to know his secret, they had to take an active part. That was the big question mark. After supper he would talk to Wife. If she agreed, he would talk to Khom.

Baby Sister greeted Chea as he fell down in exhaustion outside the hut. Looking inside, he could see that Khom was sound asleep. The quinine had saved his life. Smiling One had done his job well. He had given Chea more than he knew: awareness of the brutality that was taking place in his country and the challenge to do something about it.

As Chea ate his rice from the still warm milk can, he noticed how thin Wife had gotten. Would she be able to comprehend what he wanted to tell her? He was afraid it might be the final strain that could cause her to collapse mentally. He sat and studied her. Small, unsmiling, but still graceful, she looked like a broken sapphire. If only he could help her become what she once was. Maybe his plan would do it. Quietly he slid over to her side. She was just taking the last weed out of her rice bowl and putting it in her mouth. He had to make her understand. "I am going to escape," he whispered.

For the first time in weeks she showed some response. She turned, squinted her eyes, and stared at his face. In a second her face returned to being pale, a map of melancholy and despair. She was lost again in her own world.

"I must talk to you and you must listen. Do you understand?"

She looked down at her arm and grimaced as he squeezed it. He let go and saw the thumbprint remain. He wasn't aware he had that much strength left. "I'm sorry." Again he took her arm and held it lightly, speaking to her as he would to Baby Sister. "You must listen."

She leaned back and closed her eyes. He told her of the plan. Had she heard him? He leaned over and looked straight into her face. Feeling his breath, she opened her eyes. He held her chin and spoke in a slow, urging voice, half begging, half warning. "I must have it tomorrow, do you understand? Tomorrow! You must bring it to me."

Still no response. Chea got up and walked over to the fire. He placed his milk can by the burning embers and went in to give Khom two more quinine tablets. His son was awake now and asked for some food. Chea went out and took a milk can, put some water in it, poured in the remainder of the day's ration of rice, and stirred the fire so that it flared back up. The fact that Khom had asked for food was good news. It meant that if Wife responded and could find what he needed in the forest, then tomorrow evening he could tell his son about the plan and the part he would have to play in it.

All through the next day Chea continued to hoe, but

his activity was much slower than the day before. Because the bruises around his neck from the Smiling One's hoe handle still made swallowing difficult, he used that as an excuse to give more and more of his food to Baby Sister and Khom.

During the midday break, Wife was still uncommunicative. She gave no indication that she had gotten what he wanted nor that she planned to. He would give her the afternoon to make up her mind, and then he would have to order her to obey him. It was a chance he would have to take. Either she would break down completely, maybe go mad, or else she would do what he asked. He had to know for sure. He was too weak to keep working much longer.

The monsoons were upon them. The rain came earlier each afternoon and stayed longer. That day it seemed as if the entire yearly rainfall of 100 inches would fall before he could set his plan into action. As he made his way through the mud back to his hut, Chea assured himself that the rain would only help him. He would regard it as a special gift to send him on his way.

Khom was well enough to come out of the hut and eat his evening meal of rice, leaves, and berries. Baby Sister sat at his feet adoringly, watching her big brother scoop the food out of his milk can without dropping a grain. When she tried the same thing, most of it landed on her bare spindly legs. She would bend down, scrape up the fallen rice, and put it in her mouth—but not without giggling and a mimicked warning to herself: "You waste rice, we hit you with club."

After supper Chea laboriously stretched his infected leg in front of him. It was time to lance it again. Every couple of days large scabs and pus pockets formed. He would take a sharpened stick, pierce the pocket, and then scrape it with a sharp stone. He never went through the process without thinking of Job. It made it more bearable. The other members of the family always managed to find something to do inside the hut while he did his puncturing and scraping. When he was through, he would call Wife. She would take the can of hot water off the fire and pour it over the open wounds. He yearned for a little sulphur and a tube of the antibiotic which had been available in his village. Here, all they had was boiled stagnant water. Little wonder that the leg still throbbed day and night, causing him sleepless hours, bringing his weight down to no more than a hundred and five—fifty pounds less than the morning he left his village down the east road.

After scraping the first sore, he leaned his head back against the hut, put a stick in his mouth, and clenched his teeth. Wife, showing no signs of emotion or sympathy, poured the water slowly and methodically on the open wound. After finishing, he would sit for fifteen or twenty minutes, waiting for the pain to subside to the point where if he went to bed he could fall asleep from sheer exhaustion. Even then, the pain might still awaken him a few hours later.

Crawling into the hut he lay down beside Wife. He was always comforted by the fact that when he did so he felt warm and still needed. He reached over and touched her waist. She did not respond. He began to frame in his mind what he would say, and how he would say it. How would he react if she totally ignored him? What would he say if she started screaming? Before he could begin, Wife's hand reached over to his and stuck a leaf wrapped with grass into his palm. He knew what was inside. He lifted his head to thank her, but she lay with her eyes closed, totally immobile. He wrapped his fingers tightly around the package and crawled outside.

Khom was lying on his back in front of the hut. The

chain that once held the ivory dove, but now the sorcerer's amulet, gleamed in the moonlight. Chea edged over close to him and asked quietly, "Are you awake, son?"

There were several moments of silence before Khom answered. "Yes."

"I have something to tell you, and I want you to listen carefully."

Khom made no reply.

"I have decided to escape and get help."

Khom moved slightly.

"It is important that you know every detail because you are going to have to help me. Do you understand?"

"I understand," answered Khom in his usual monotone, not moving.

Chea explained what he was going to do. Khom listened, not making a sound. "Will you help me?" Chea asked.

"Yes," said Khom. "I will help."

Again, as with Wife, Chea looked for some sign of acceptance, some indication that at least one string of the relationship had been retied. Khom rolled over on his side as if to go to sleep.

Chea crawled back into the hut and tried to rest. He had hoped that sharing his plan would take away some of the disquietude he felt. It didn't. Hour after hour he rehearsed every move, practicing breathing through his mouth so that his stomach didn't move and his nostrils didn't flare. He placed his hand tightly over his mouth and nose, holding his breath as long as he could, letting go only when he began to feel as if he would pass out. He counted—first twenty seconds, then twenty-four. He was getting better.

In the morning Khom was well enough to go to work. As he was about to leave, his father whispered, "I'll take the herbs and seeds after the noon meal.

Then I'll ask them to bring me back when they take effect.''

Khom nodded a noncommittal understanding.

Chea noticed that Wife had heard what he said. She stood motionless for a few seconds. Then she slowly made her way to the forest for another morning of work.

The morning went by slowly. Chea noticed neither the sun nor the early rain. All he could think about was where he would be tomorrow at this time. The morning passed and Chea returned to the hut. As he approached, he picked up a milk can of water before going inside. Baby Sister was there. He asked her to go help Mommy prepare food. With her usual cheerfulness, she quickly obeyed, and Chea was alone. Carefully he dug a little dirt from the corner of the hut and took out the package. He untied the grass string, opened it on the ground, and separated the six seeds from the four herbs. The seeds he pushed aside. He knew how *ply slyng* worked; it would make him violently ill about thirty minutes after he took it. The *krik* herb was different. He had no idea how much of it to take. All he knew was that the witch doctors in his village had once used it to cast spells. They would sneak it into food. A couple of hours later the victim's temperature would rise, and his body would shake convulsively. Every indication was that he was struck by a severe case of malaria. The witch doctors called it a hex, and it gave them great power. If you used too much, you never had to take any more. Your heart stopped. It was now Chea's plan to take the herb in an amount he had yet to decide. Then, just before going to the field, he would take the *ply slyng*. After working for a short time, he would get violently ill. His fever would go up, and a couple of workers would carry him home with what they thought was malaria. When Wife got home she would give him a dosage of herb which he would have set aside. His heart would slow down, and he would almost, but not quite, lose consciousness. Khom would tell a soldier that his father was dead. The soldier already knowing he was sick, would come over, take a look a Chea, and maybe even take his pulse to verify that he was dead.

His son was then to take him to the graveyard, put him in an especially shallow grave that he would dig today, cover him with dirt and leaves, and come home. After dark, Chea would crawl out of his grave and escape into the forest. In the morning, Khom would throw more leaves on the grave to fill up the hole. No one would know that his father wasn't buried there at all, but was making his way through the forest to get help from Thailand.

Rehearsing it in his mind one last time, Chea broke off a piece of the herb and wrapped it back up in the leaf. This is what Wife would give him later in the evening when she returned from the forest.

As he would have done for a meal, Chea took the piece of herb, bowed his head, and quickly threw it in his mouth. He washed it down with a mouthful of water. That done, he got up, walked out of the hut, and took the rice that had been prepared for him. As Wife handed it to him, he in turn handed her the remaining herb which she tucked into her waistband. Khom watched.

The meal was eaten and it was time to return to work. Chea reached under the tucking of his *sampot*, or what was left of it, and took out four seeds. He put them in his mouth and drank a can of water. Without looking at Wife or Khom, he got up and headed for the field.

Two hours later, from the graveyard where he was digging a special grave, Khom saw three men carrying someone in a horizontal position toward the hut.

Without consideration for his apparent condition,

79

the men dumped Chea in front of his hut and went back to the field. Chea clasped his stomach, retching. His head was swimming. He was afraid he would pass out. The old woman who took care of the children in the unit sat at the next hut watching, offering neither help nor advice. If he died tonight, his unit would still get his rice ration for tomorrow. She and the others could use it. Baby Sister came running around the corner and saw her father rolling on the ground. She began to cry. The last thing he remembered was Little Sister pouring water on his sore leg. "Daddy sick, Daddy sick, Little Sister will make Daddy well."

Wife returned from the field to find her husband lying on his back outside the hut, burning with a fever and near the point of delirium. Every few minutes he would regain some clarity and stare at her. Finally he mustered the strength to tell her to give him the rest of the herb.

Looking up through glazed eyes, he thought he saw Khom standing beside him, but he wasn't sure. Wife hesitated in getting the remaining herb. He tried to whisper, "Please," then sank into unconsciousness again. The next thing he knew, Wife was holding his head up. He could feel the herb hit his tongue, followed by a sip of water. The nausea had passed, but there was terrible pain in his head and chest. He had heard that this was how people felt before they died from a cobra bite. Had he overdosed? For the next hour he moved back and forth between consciousness and unconsciousness. He opened his eyes once and leaning over him was a soldier. He felt someone take his hand, feel his pulse, and then a voice said, "You can bury him in the morning. Right now, you have to attend a re-indoctrination meeting. Go, quickly." The tone of the soldier's voice indicated that if Khom and Wife didn't move at once, the soldier would use his club.

Chea wanted to scream, "No, bury me now! I'm

dead, bury me now!" If they didn't bury him until tomorrow, he would have to lie in that grave all day under the hot sun and driving rain. If he didn't die from the heat, he would drown.

Chea heard people talking, but he couldn't communicate with them. He was unable to move. Was he really dead, was this that moment before the spirit left the body?

The whispered voice of Khom broke through the silence. "Look, Mother, can't you see? Father never had any plans to escape out there in the forest. He wanted to escape through death. He has committed suicide. He went the way of a coward."

Chea heard no more. He lay paralyzed. He had to come back to tell them it wasn't true. He had to tell them he really was going to escape. Darkness engulfed him but he would not give up. He began to see himself as a child. He talked to his dead mother and father. Things long forgotten passed before him as the pain and apprehension subsided.

Slowly Chea began to move his lips, but words would not come out. Dirt fell into his mouth. He tried to lift one arm, but he was too weak. He tried lifting his leg, but there was a heavy weight on it. One arm was lying at his side, the other over his chest. He fought to get his breath. The stench was unbearable. A wave of nausea swept over him. Gradually he moved his arm up the side, pushing against what felt like dirt. He touched leaves, and then he froze as he felt something else. He wasn't sure what it was. Was it his wife lying beside him in bed? Was he having a dream that he couldn't breathe? Continuing his limited movement, he gasped as he realized what was on top of him. Another person's body. He was in a grave, and they had thrown another body on top of him. He didn't know whether to shout for help or die quietly. Then he remembered his son's words, "He has committed suicide. He went the way of a coward." The idea infused new strength into his wracked system. Gradually he continued to dig out with one hand.

As he lay thinking about what to do next, a rumble blocked out all his thoughts. Was he about to be run over by a tank or a truck? Water began to trickle over his face, and he lost consciousness. As he awakened, he tried to remember what had happened. Was it morning? No, it had to be evening, because the day's rain had come. Then he realized that the water was rising in his grave. If he didn't get out soon, he would drown. The rain had washed away much of the dirt around and under him and had lifted him up, pressing him more firmly against the body that was above him. As nearly as he could figure out, it was a child.

He began to ask himself questions. "Should I make one leap and try to get out of the grave? But what if it's still daylight? I would be seen, and then I would really be dead, along with Khom, Wife, and Baby Sister."

The rain kept coming down. He knew he had to move or drown. The cool water gave him strength and revived him mentally. He tried to roll over on his side. The dead body slid to one side. He was now covered by what he hoped were only leaves. He lifted his head a little at a time, trying to get his eyes into the open as quickly as possible to see if he had exposed himself. There was no light. He was revolted by the stench of putrefied flesh. Was it his? Was it the child buried on top of him? Suddenly he realized that it was the smell of the graveyard. His head was protruding out of his grave into the pitch black night. The rain began to let up.

Early the next morning Khom came back and spoke to his mother. "The grave has sunk a little, but not much. It doesn't look like it's been disturbed. It was full of water. If he wasn't dead, he is now." He spat on the ground. Wife moved quickly into the hut.

EIGHT

Chea leaned against a tree. He was sitting in a puddle of water with rain running down his face. He wasn't sure where he was, but he vaguely recalled having crawled through grass and bushes. He had no idea which direction he had come from. All that mattered was being out of the camp and away from the smell of death.

The exhilaration of freedom quickly subsided into despair. He looked at his emaciated body. He reached down and touched his swollen leg. "What's the use?" he thought. "That will turn to gangrene in a few days, and I'll die anyway." He felt rebellion welling up inside. "Why didn't I drown? What difference would it have made?"

He picked up some twigs and threw them against the ground. "What's back there, anyway? A wife who lives in another world. A son who thinks his father is a coward." His head fell on his chest. He closed his eyes and bit his bottom lip. He sucked in his breath in an attempt to regain control.

Looking down, he noticed a small leaf protruding from the fold of his *sampot*. He reached down and took it out. It was a small banana leaf, bound with grass. He had neither seen it nor felt it before.

With trembling hands he untied it. He broke one of the pieces of grass and the contents spilled out onto his lap. Carefully he reached down and picked it up. As though he were handling a pearl of great price, he tenderly took the folded white scarf and held it to his lips. His nose picked up the faint scent of perfume. His shoulders began to heave, as with both hands he held the scarf to his face and wept.

Thoughts that were too intimate to speak fed new strength into his body. He folded the white scarf, placed it back inside the leaf, and bound it again with a piece of grass. He was a husband again. He was needed.

The sun broke through the clouds. The rain was through. The shadows cast by the trees indicated that it was early afternoon. He could watch the shadows as they lengthened and then he would know in which direction to travel.

The reality of the need for food caused him to look around. He reached over his shoulder to the tree trunk and pulled off a piece of bark. Without looking at it, he shoved it into his mouth and chewed. If it had any food value, he would need it. If it didn't, at least it would help to fill his stomach. He turned his head to the tree for more, and his eye caught something moving. A few inches from him, coming out from under its rain shelter, was a worm about two inches long and the diameter of his index finger. He turned his head in the other direction. He needed protein. He needed food, he told himself, and there it was.

Without looking, he swept his hand over the ground until he touched something warm. It moved, trying to get away. He picked it up between his thumb and index finger, threw his head back, and dropped it into his mouth. Gagging, he closed his mouth and swallowed. He quickly grabbed another piece of bark and began chewing on it. He had done it! There was no taste. All he had to do was keep his mind from probing his stomach, reminding him of what was down there.

His eye caught sight of some more protein, about the same size, wiggling its way toward the tree. He repeated the process.

He leaned back and took deep breaths of cool air. The nausea subsided for a moment, and then returned. He put his head between his knees and closed his eyes. In a few moments he opened them and saw another worm crawling out of a small pile of bark. He let it go. A little protein is better than none, he told himself. He realized he was smiling. It had been a long time.

He got up on one knee to test both his strength and the reaction of his stomach. The legs were ready, but his stomach wasn't. Again he placed his head between his knees, continuing to breathe deeply. He enjoyed the fresh air, not violated by the stench of rotting bodies, excrement, sweat, and the other smells of this "liberated" nation.

As he brought his head up, he noticed shadows beginning to stretch across a small clearing. Now he had his directions clear. That was west and that was east. Thailand is that way, he told himself. He struggled to get to his feet. Thailand was over there, a long walk.

His knees buckled for a second, but then he stood. A wave of nausea again swept over him, but disappeared after a few deep breaths. He turned and with uncertain step began his journey.

He traveled about an hour, staying away from clearings. His feet and his injured leg were bleeding. He sat down to rest, leaning against a fallen log. As he looked at his swollen leg he noticed that he would not have to find a stick to puncture the infected areas; his walk through the underbrush had done the job for him.

Lying down, he looked through the trees to the sky,

spoke a few words, and went to sleep. He dreamed of roast pork, one of his favorite dishes. He had not had any since that fateful morning. He imagined himself reaching across the table, picking up a large piece, mixing it with sauce, and dropping it into his mouth. He suddenly woke up and realized it was only a dream. His stomach and head were aching. He gritted his teeth and laid his head back against the log.

He sniffed once, then again. He pinched his good leg. He wasn't asleep, but still he smelled meat cooking. He sat up and turned his head, trying to find the smell again. A little to the right. Like an animal seeking out food, he got to his knees and began to crawl, slowly, quietly, in the darkness. He ran into a log and rolled himself over it. His head hit a tree. The pitch dark night offered no guidance. He raised up a little at a time, cautiously. Halfway up, the smell was unmistakable. There was no doubt; it wasn't a dream. He stood up and leaned his shoulder against a tree. After a few moments, he continued to follow the aroma that wafted through the forest, mixing with the smell of rotting leaves and bark.

Suddenly he thought he saw a light through some branches. He dropped to his knees, his arms at his sides.

The moon was coming out from under a cloud and he began to see the silhouette of the forest. He lay down on his stomach, carefully lifted his head, and again saw a momentary flash of light.

Was it a loggers' camp? Were they American soldiers on their way to free his people? Excitement overtook him, and he had to remind himself that it might be neither. Breathing heavily, he began to crawl toward the light.

He stopped. Voices. Someone laughed. He couldn't catch the language. He rolled himself over a log and slid under a clump of bushes. He looked out into a small clearing and saw the forms of several people sitting around a fire. Over the fire an animal, probably a wild pig, was being roasted. Chea was ready to get up and run to them, joining their feast, when a figure stood and stirred the fire. Flames leapt up, and he could see the black pajama uniforms and AK-17s of the Khmer Rouge. The aroma was almost unbearable. The pain in his stomach increased. One of the men removed the bayonet from his rifle to cut pieces from whatever was roasting. Once in awhile Chea would hear laughter. Although he was too far away to hear what they were saying, occasionally he caught some disconnected Khmer word.

The fire began to grow dim as they continued to eat. The aroma disappeared. The fire died. The moon silhouetted ten or fifteen soldiers sleeping on the ground.

If he didn't get some food soon, he would die. Should he try for it? The foolishness of the idea became clear as he felt the wrapped leaf tucked into his *sampot*. He had to think of more than himself. He would wait until morning and, when the soldiers left, he would scrape the bones.

Hours passed. The moon went behind a cloud, then reappeared, always revealing the same picture. No one in the camp moved.

Without some form of manufactured protection, man is a coward, Chea thought. Not many can conquer when stripped of their machinery, guns, clubs, and rockets. Chea recalled the words his father was so fond of quoting after giving him a lesson in the importance of turning the other cheek. "The only reason we fight each other is because we are not brave enough to live without war—nor do we want to take the time to nurture a reasonable alternative." How many of those young soldiers knew anything but war? He felt pity for them. He wouldn't want to change places with them, food or no food.

His thoughts turned to his own son. Khom would welcome him back as a father. Such thoughts solidified his physical and mental strength. He was ready for another day. His eyes closed. His body relaxed, sinking into the leaves behind a rotting log.

Sounds awakened him. It was daylight and the soldiers were moving out. Would they finish off the meat for breakfast? Would they walk in his direction? Would he be found? He looked over the log and watched as they moved about. Several of them talked in groups while gnawing on leftover bones. One threw his bone to the ground and pointed to a spot near Chea's clump of bushes. The soldiers began to walk single file, coming closer. None of them spoke. Chea watched, transfixed. They could have been the "visitors" that came to his village. Their uniforms were the same, only these had rubber thongs made of used automobile tires. The others had been barefoot. With their AK-17s slung over their shoulders, the tattered contingent walked by, no more than three feet from Chea. He lay close to the log until the sound of footsteps gradually faded.

It took all Chea's mental strength not to jump up and run to the abandoned campsite. Maybe the soldiers knew he was there and wanted to set a trap for him. Rather than just walking over and killing him, they perhaps wanted something with more sport to it. Is that what they were talking about when the one pointed in his direction?

Chea erased those possibilities from his mind by beginning slowly to count. When he reached one thousand he would make his way, in a circular route, to the campsite and perhaps to some food—or to death.

He started counting, one, two, three, tapping his

finger three times between each number. By the time
he reached five hundred, his finger was tired and his
tempo had increased. At eight hundred fifty, he
crawled out from under the bush and inched his way
on his knees toward the camp. He made a half circle,
ending up behind the site, and then crawled directly
toward it. Every few feet he stopped and listened for
voices, breaking twigs, or gunfire.

Though he had quit counting, he imagined he would
have reached three thousand by the time he arrived at
the back side of the camp. His knees were bleeding and
one hand was full of thorns. The only pain he felt was
in his stomach. He rose slowly, looking in the direction in which the soldiers had gone.

He could see his former hiding place. He had been
only about thirty feet from the soldiers' abandoned
campsite. He could see pieces of something scattered
around, but he wasn't sure they were food. He returned
to his knees and began crawling toward the site. A
boar's head was lying beside the dead campfire. He
stood up and headed for the pig's head. He fell down
beside it, picked it up with both hands, and started to
chew on it. Nearby lay a leg bone. He picked it up and
sat down behind a tree. Meticulously he picked off
slivers of meat, placing them on his tongue and slowly
chewing them.

Finally, all that could be picked or chewed off the leg
was gone. Only a few hairs remained, along with the
unchewable hoof.

He found two other legs, some pieces of meat, and
tied them around his waist with some grass. He still
had a dangerous journey ahead of him. He realized that
the food in his stomach could not yet have fueled the
hungry furnace that his body had become, but psycho-
logically he now was ready to move on. He was certain
he remembered the general direction in which he
should head. Cautiously he stood and began making

his way through the forest toward the west, the Thailand border, and help.

After several hours of travel, and a short stop at a running stream where he washed his wounds and drank his fill of water, he noticed that the forest was getting thicker. He was coming to the bottom of the mountain range "over which the clouds circle." Because this was about where two ranges met, he guessed that it would not be more than one thousand feet high.

He felt reasonably sure that he would not run into any more Khmer Rouge. They, like most of his people, feared the forest because many evil spirits were supposed to live there. It was a superstition that Chea was certain had not been demolished by whatever other incentives the "organization" had promised their young executioners. Even the Khmer Rouge knew that all evil spirits were imbued with the potent *tik thanam kong,* a potion made of dried python, excrement from the nest of a red vulture, and red water. This potion was thought to make the spirits invulnerable to the penetration of a spear, knife, or bullet, thus making the soldiers' AK-17s useless in the spirit world. Chea was saddened that people would believe such superstitions, but he was glad that they helped in keeping the Khmer Rouge out of the forests while he made his way to Thailand.

Several hours later, as the sun began to skim across the treetops, the heavily wooded area he had been traveling through came to an abrupt end. Chea looked into a huge clearing where for several years a lumber company had ravaged the mountainside. There had been no attempt to reforest, or to stop erosion. Large gullies were being cut out of the hillside by the rains. On the other side of the clearing, standing out against a clouded sky, was his mountain. To get there now, he would have to expose himself in broad daylight, a chance he dared not take. He went back a few yards into the forest, lay down, took a boar's foot from around his waist, and chewed on the gristle. His stomach satisfied, he set the bone aside and fell asleep.

When he awoke, he was momentarily disoriented. It was raining and the sky was black. He had to review the day quickly in his mind so that he would know where he was. He remembered the mountain, the clearing. Which direction was it? He got up and moved around the bushes. His eyes began to adjust to the darkness, and he was certain that the clearing was straight ahead. Without hesitation, he started to walk. He had only gone a little way when he realized he was crossing a road. He remembered seeing it at the bottom of the gully earlier in the day. He now was certain he was heading in the right direction. He quickened his pace and headed into the clearing.

It wasn't long before he realized it was becoming more difficult to walk and he was getting very tired. He sat down for a moment and started to slide down the rain-soaked hillside. Only then did he realize that he had been climbing the mountain.

He began to climb again. The terrain was sometimes almost level, then suddenly it turned to an angle again. Sometimes he was on his knees, other times erect. The rain had stopped, but the moon had not yet come through the clouds. Some inner strength kept him moving. He forgot about the boar's leg tied around his waist. He forgot about the Khmer Rouge. Nothing mattered except getting to the top of the mountain where he was sure he would see the border and find help.

As the night progressed, the moon would come out for short intervals, like someone holding a flashlight every so often to show him which way to travel and where to step. Gradually, he felt less strain on his legs. More and more he walked erect. He threw aside the stick he had picked up to help him climb. The moon came out between two clouds. He looked down and saw nothing but darkness. He looked up and saw circling clouds in the night sky.

He had reached the summit.

Chea fell to the ground and breathed heavily. All the energy drained out of him in both exhilaration and fatigue from his self-imposed forced march. In a few minutes he got up, walked around, and discovered a tree stump. He sat down and leaned against it, wishing it still had leaves to protect him from the heavy drizzle.

He untied another of the boar's legs from his waist and began chewing on it. For a moment the drizzle stopped. The moon shone through the haze and again he could see the darkness below and the light above. He stopped chewing as the moon began slowly to lose itself in the rain clouds. He was enveloped in a pitch-black mist. There was no light anywhere. He could not see even the boar's leg before him.

A great darkness crept over him. Food no longer mattered and he set it down. The darkness from below had crawled up his mountain and encircled him. He reached down into the tuck of his *sampot* and took out the banana leaf. Unfolding it, he again held the white scarf to his face. The slight smell of perfume was gone. It was only a piece of white cloth.

Not since his wedding night had he so desired to be with his wife. Never before had he so longed for her presence. Tears welled up in his eyes as he said her name softly, "Douang Kolab." How long had it been since he had called her by name? Always it was Wife. He even thought of her in that way—not as a unique person, but as an automaton in a role.

Though he had never been unfaithful to her, he had still given her terrible pain. He looked up to the sky, now black as the valley below. Heavy mist continued to settle on his body and he began to shiver. Outwardly he cursed the blindness that had brought him here, but inwardly he was thankful. He wanted to speak her name again, but choked. He murmured quietly, "Kolab, my Kolab," and then spoke to himself. "Like my tools at work, she is something to turn off and turn on. When I want a stone, I turn her on and she gives me a precious jewel so that other people can admire my workmanship."

The same terrible depression that had settled over Chea when he heard Clerk cry out for his massacred son again wrenched him. It came to him that Kolab was never a part of those early morning hours he, in a better day, had guarded so jealously and had been so proud of. His dreams, his plans, were all for Chea.

"I did admire her beauty," he told himself. "I often told her that. I never thought of the beauty as hers, but always mine. She gave her beauty to me to shape, to mold, to add to, to become one with, and I kept it and never gave it back. I called it mine, and let it rot in my hands. Oh, Douang Kolab, Douang Kolab," he cried. "No wonder you hate me. No wonder Khom hates me. Your only hope in life was Pha, and when she died, you had no one else to share yourself with. And so, you died as well. What is beauty if there is no one to share it with? What good is a sapphire if no one ever sees it? What good is a person if no one ever sees her?"

Thirteen years came flooding over Chea. His chest ached. His head throbbed. His eyes burned. And then, again, he brought the white scarf to his nose and lips. Whether real or imagined, the scent of perfume wafted through his nostrils, his heart grew peaceful, warm tears washed his eyes. Now he understood. He spoke a promise aloud to the mist which was now clearing, to the light now shining about.

The sun shining in his eyes awoke Chea with a start. He had slept through the dawn. He lifted his head, removed the scarf from his face, and blinked several times. He rubbed his eyes and stared in disbelief. Below him was the green valley, a road, the river, and then the border which ran into the azure sky. Even aside from all the emotions of his new experience, of his new realization, the beauty was inexpressible, yet he realized it was not separate from last night, but part of it.

He squeezed the white scarf in his hand and wished that his Kolab were here to enjoy it with him. She would find just the right word to describe it. With that thought, he smiled to himself, realizing that last night was not a dream, but an event. He no longer felt the same. Now the mist had lifted, the darkness had vanished, and he could see freedom just across the river.

Quickly he rewrapped the white scarf and tucked it into his *sampot*. He ate another part of the boar's leg. His trip from here on would be downhill, but much more dangerous. The closer he got to the border, the more Khmer Rouge soldiers there would be. He had heard rumors that the borders were all closed, that anyone caught trying to cross was shot without warning.

With that thought in mind, he began to walk down the side of the small mountain, which looked much less formidable from the top than from the bottom. He headed for the nearest vegetation, knowing he must stay under cover at all times and wait until dark to cross the river.

He had traveled for about an hour when he came to a small clearing. A quarter of a mile away he could see a road. But that was not all. He fell down flat on his stomach and raised his head cautiously so as to see through the clearing to the road. Over to his left was a group of about thirty men, women, and children, who were making their way to the border. Around a curve in the road, about ten Khmer Rouge with weapons over their shoulders were walking, in single file, toward the refugees.

Chea felt the same as he had on that day when the men had been tied to the tree with the plastic bags over their heads. Should he stand and scream, "Run, run," or was the outcome inevitable, no matter what he did? He watched the refugees move closer to the bend in the road from one side, and the Khmer Rouge soldiers from the other. He raised himself up and started to shout a warning. Gunfire drowned out any sound.

It all was familiar to Chea. The staccato, short bursts of the rifles, women and children screaming, and then silence. Several soldiers walked among the victims, bayoneting the dead and dying. There were to be no survivors. Chea put his head down in the dirt, unable to move.

When he looked up again he could see the last Khmer disappearing down the road. Directly below him the road was strewn with bodies.

Chea knew that his people were afraid of the dead. That was why the soldiers would always leave the bodies and move on, or insist that they be buried at once. This meant that he now had safe passage across the road. It also meant that he would have to cross where the bodies lay. He was not afraid of the dead, but the idea still lingered that perhaps he could have saved some had he given them warning.

He rose from his hiding place and half slid down the side of the mountain. Now he was glad his Kolab was not with him. She had seen enough death. She needed no more reminders of human cruelty.

Soon he found himself at the side of the road. He tried not to look as he crossed. Then he stopped in the middle. A few feet away he saw what was once a beautiful young mother with hair to her shoulders and swollen feet. A dead child lay under her, and there was a bayonet hole in her back. Not far away lay a boy about twelve years old, one foot across another's body, his face buried in the dirt.

All the strength that Chea had regained dissolved in a second. He put his hands over his face and let out a moan. Slowly he moved over to the young mother. He knelt beside her on one knee. Gently he took her hair and turned her head aside. She was a stranger, as were the child on her back and the young boy. He hoped that her husband had loved her before it had been too late. He got up and walked swiftly across the road and into the forest. No looking back.

By early afternoon he had made his way through the underbrush, entangled vines, and several clearings. He had run, walked, crawled on his knees and belly, but he had finally made it to the riverbank. He knew he couldn't attempt to cross until after dark. It had already rained some, and would continue through the afternoon. He found himself a place under some bushes and lay down, studying the small river below, and on the other side, the Thai border.

Doubts began to bombard his mind. What if this was the wrong river? What if he had gone in the wrong direction? What if the soldiers used flares at night, as was rumored?

The rains subsided for a few minutes. Then his body tensed as he heard music. It didn't sound familiar, and it was coming straight toward him. As he lay there, four Khmer soldiers walked along the river just below him, looking across to the other side. One of them carried what appeared to be a small cassette tape player, the kind he had seen before in his village. He could hear the words and music, a song he had heard both Pha and Khom sing around the house. The soldiers were like his children. He thought of the incongruity of it all. Four young soldiers, carrying AK-17s they had probably used to kill innumerable people, walking through the forest playing a song from America. The words wafted across the trees. One of the soldiers was swaying his body in tempo to the music, as the one behind him laughed and sang the words in English. "Maybe there is hope for these kids after all," Chea thought, "if the right people could get to them. If somehow the faceless monsters from the 'organization' that sent them on their mission could be exposed, maybe this senseless massacre would end." It gave Chea new hope for his own son.

Darkness fell and the rains let up. "Now is the time," he told himself. "The greater the danger, the greater the reward." He slid into the swift current. Swimming took different muscles than walking through the forest. In a few moments he felt himself being carried downstream. He struggled ashore again on the side from which he had started—and closer to the soldiers who had gone by earlier.

Crawling back into the water, he tried again. This time he would swim upstream. Before long the current pulled him under. He thought of all the times he had craved water while on the forced march, in the fields planting corn, in the middle of the night, in the grave. And now he was drowning!

If he had any reserve power, this was the time to use it. He tried again to bring both arms up and swim upstream, but the current was too strong. He started rolling like a log. Making one last effort to gain control, he suddenly felt something solid. Both feet dug into mud. He stood halfway up and looked around in disbelief. He was drowning in four feet of water! Holding his head down, he dropped to his knees and crawled into some bushes on the bank. A huge flare lit the sky and the river. The place where he had just been was lit up like midday. Across the way he could see four soldiers, their weapons pointed at the water. Their tape machine was not playing. The flare hovered for a few minutes and then plunged into the water, leaving behind the darkness it had invaded. Chea crawled deeper into the underbrush, trying to plan what he would do next. He was across the river, but not at the border.

He ticked off in his mind the things to watch for. There could be mine fields. He would have to crawl part of the way. He would have to guess the right direction. It was possible to travel parallel to the border and never know it. Finally, he would have to stand and make a run for it.

There would be Khmer Rouge soldiers out there with only one purpose: to kill anyone they caught in the no-man's land between the land of fratricide and the land of friendship.

He began to crawl out from the underbrush. It was raining, but less than before. After crawling on his stomach until his arms refused to drag him any more, he stopped and sat up. He was ready to take a chance on making a run for it. The rain let up and he could see light about a quarter of a mile straight ahead. Thailand?

Crouching down, he walked slowly. The rain started again and, taking advantage of the poor visibility, he broke into a run. Rain came down in sheets. The harder it rained, the faster he ran. Suddenly he fell into a deep pool of water. The river? Had he been running in the wrong direction?

The rain stopped for a moment. Another flare lit the sky. He held his head under the water until he began to pass out. Raising his head, he took a deep breath. The flare died. He could see he was lying in a small ditch full of water. In his confusion he had mistaken a small irrigation ditch for a river. Just ahead of him were the lights.

He crawled out of the ditch and on his hands and

knees kept moving toward the light. A couple of soldiers were walking around with weapons slung over their shoulders. Should he go around or keep on in the same direction?

With his bleeding elbows pulling him, and bloody knees pushing, he edged closer to investigate. The rain had almost stopped. The moon was beginning to break through the clouds. He could hear several men talking. Then he heard children laughing. Some others were singing in Cambodian. He recognized the song. "Amazing grace, how sweet the sound, that saved a wretch like me . . ." He stood up and walked toward the music. Voices trailed off in mid-sentence, the guitar player stopped strumming, everyone turned to look at the dirty, bloody mess standing there in front of them. Several women gasped. Men drew their breath through their teeth. One came walking from the front of the room, put his arm around Chea, and said in his own language, "Don't be frightened. This is a Cambodian refugee camp. You are safe here."

As he fell into a chair, the guitar started strumming and the singers gradually joined in: "I once was lost, but now am found. . . ."

NINE

Chea sat on the side of a table and sipped hot tea while a doctor injected him with an antibiotic and then spread salve over his swollen leg. Chea looked the doctor over. "Probably about my age," thought Chea, "a little heavier." His analysis of the doctor was interrupted by pain as bandages were applied to his left knee, slit open from crawling on it. Both elbows were bandaged as well.

Someone had brought him a new *sampot* and laid it out beside him. What was left of the old one had been neatly folded and put on a table across the room. A leaf bound with grass lay on top of it. A new pair of thongs were set beside the *sampot*. Several people who had been at the meeting he had interrupted were standing by, watching the Thai doctor. Another came in and laid a clean white shirt beside the new *sampot*. The doctor took a small stick with cotton on the end and dabbed a pink medicine on small wounds and scratches on his arms, legs, and stomach.

"There," said the doctor as he set the stick aside and stepped back to look at his patient. "Now, all you need is a little rest." He reached over to the nurse and took a syringe from her hand. With one practiced move the doctor squirted a little fluid in the air and, without breaking the rhythm, stuck it into Chea's arm. Chea let out a short gasp, more from surprise than pain. "That will help you rest," said the doctor as he turned to set the syringe on a table. Chea felt his head begin to spin and he felt terribly tired. Quietly he began to slide off the table. The doctor and another man took hold of his arms and helped him to a small mat on the floor.

Chea looked around the empty room, and then smiled as quiet darkness from outside closed around him.

"How are you feeling?" The doctor was standing over him, looking down with a smile.

"Good, I think," Chea replied as he tried to lift himself up from the mat. The brightness of the daylight kept him from opening his eyes completely.

"Maybe you better lie there for awhile," said the doctor as he put his hand on Chea's shoulder. "You are all right here. This is the refugee camp infirmary. I'll have some food brought to you." The doctor left the room and Chea fell back on the mat.

In a few minutes, a young Cambodian woman arrived with a bowl of hot soup, filled with fish. She knelt down beside Chea and handed it to him, then left the room as unobtrusively as she had entered.

Chea sat up, took the bowl in both hands and drank it, chewing the bits of fish and relishing every bite.

"Better not eat too much, too fast; your system is going to take awhile to get used to it." Again the doctor stood over him. Chea ignored his advice and finished off the bowl of soup. He set the empty bowl on the floor beside him. The doctor asked if he felt well enough to stand up.

Chea said he did, and with the help of the wall and the doctor, he got to a chair.

"What happened to your leg?" asked the doctor.

Chea explained with as little detail as possible and then asked the doctor, "Where can I go to see the military leader here?"

"The military leader? This is a refugee camp, not a military camp."

"Then how far away is the military camp? I have to see a Thai military officer, one who has authority. One who can talk to the prime minister of Thailand if necessary."

"Maybe you had just better talk to me for a few days," counseled the doctor in his best bedside manner.

"No," said Chea, his voice rising. "No." He attempted to stand up. "I must talk to the military."

The doctor put his hand on his shoulder and said quietly, "All right, you just sit down and rest for a few minutes and I'll talk to one of the guards. In the meantime, let me give you a shot to relax you."

Chea moved away. "No. I didn't come here to sleep. I came to get help." Chea attempted to back away.

"You and eighteen thousand others," said the doctor with a trace of impatience as he walked out of the room. Soon he returned with a man in a military uniform.

"I understand that you want to talk to the military." The soldier looked at him, sat down, and then stared at him. "Well, talk," said the soldier in broken Khmer.

"Sir," said Chea as he attempted to stand more erect. "I have traveled across the mountains to get help. My people are back there, and I promised them that I would bring back Thai and American troops. If I don't hurry, they will all be shot or clubbed to death."

"Sir," replied the soldier, repeating Chea's politeness, "how long has it been since you have read a newspaper?"

"Not since before Phnom Penh fell," Chea replied.

"Then maybe you should come over to our office and I will show you some."

The soldier looked at the doctor and the doctor nodded. "But have him back here in a couple of hours. He needs some more work on that leg."

Chea followed the soldier across the refugee camp which was made up of a series of long houses accommodating several thousand. They passed a large community kitchen, and then a playground for the children. A few stood back to stare. Several children fell in behind the bedraggled, gaunt man with his mission to save Cambodia.

Chea was beginning to breathe heavily and feel nauseated when, to his relief, the soldier led him into a small room equipped with several shortwave receivers, a desk, and two chairs. The soldier motioned him to take a seat and handed him that morning's newpaper. "Let's take this one for a starter," he said.

Chea looked at the headlines. He read as well as understood the Thai language, and the words nearly knocked him off his chair: ALL U.S. TROOPS TO LEAVE THAILAND.

"But what about Vietnam? Can't we get help from there?"

"Vietnam fell to the communists six weeks after your country fell."

"Laos?" inquired Chea, moving to the edge of his chair. "The U.S.? How about the U.S.?"

The soldier opened his drawer and handed him a copy of an older newspaper. It was apparent that he had read it many times. Chea reached for it and read, first out loud, and then to himself.

> ... Ambassador Dean Bunker flew out of Phnom Penh on April 12, 1976, carrying with him an American flag that flew over the U.S. embassy

in Phnom Penh, and a letter from the Cambodian head of state, Sirik Matak. He had offered Matak a ride to "freedom" but instead the chief of the crumbling empire that had withstood 600 years of foreign intervention gave the Ambassador a letter. It was Matak's last will and testament, and the Khmer Rouge later took him from the French embassy and executed him . . .

Chea read on in disbelief. All the old pains returned to his body. The tree, the plastic bags, the massacre on the road were all superimposed over the words, which he read silently. Each word was like a knife cutting off a new piece of flesh.

I thank you very sincerely for your letter and your offer to transport us toward freedom. I cannot leave, alas, leave in such a cowardly fashion. As for you, and in particular, your great country, I never believed for a moment that you would have this feeling of abandoning people which had chosen liberty. You have refused us your protection and we can do nothing about it. You leave, and my wish is that you and your country will find happiness under the sky. But mark it well, that if I shall die here on the spot in my country which I love, it is not too bad because we are all born and must die one day. I have committed this mistake in believing in the Americans. Signed: Sirik Matak, The Republic of Cambodia.

Chea looked up at the soldier, then back at the newspaper. He folded it neatly and put it back on the desk. He stood and began to make his way to the door. The soldier had traces of tears in his eyes. "I'm sorry to have bothered you," said Chea, as he shook his hand. The soldier stood as Chea walked out, his eyes following him to the door.

Chea made his way back to the clinic. No medicine could help what he felt inside. He had not only read an epistle of indictment against the country he had always loved and trusted, but he had also read his life story. Only he was not Sirik Matak. Sirik was a hero. Chea was sure he wasn't.

Quietly he went into the doctor's office and sat down on a chair. The doctor came in a few minutes and started to take the bandage off his swollen leg.

"This is going to hurt," he said softly, beginning to remove the bandage. The nurse left the room. The doctor put a mask over his nose. Chea felt nothing.

The doctor finished changing the bandage, stood up, and said, "Someone will be here in a few minutes to take you to one of the barracks. They have made room for you with some of the people who brought you in last night."

Chea uttered a feeble "Thank you."

The doctor handed him some pills. "Here, take these. They will kill some of the pain."

When the doctor left, Chea dropped the little brown envelope between the slats in the floor. The pain he felt could not be anesthetized out of existence.

A short time later, he was lying on his mat in one of the long sheds. A man about his own age, who had escorted him to his living quarters, explained camp life—what time to eat, where to wash, where the toilets were located—and gave him other information. He ended with an admonition: "Remember, no one is allowed to leave the camp without permission."

Chea thanked him, but said no more. He wanted to be alone. Grief came over him as he thought about his wife. "How many times had Kolab felt the same way—lost, alone, betrayed, ignored." He had been too concerned about business, about how people would react. "Is this revenge?" he thought.

Chea ignored both the call to lunch and supper. He got up only once, to relieve himself. Several people came by to talk to him, but he heard nothing they said. From a distance he could hear singing.

The next morning he accepted the offer to join his escort for breakfast. Together they lined up, each holding a tray on which a nourishing breakfast was placed. His companion nodded to the server, and Chea was given an extra helping. He thought of all those still back in his country.

Someone from the next table walked over and spoke to his companion. "The journalists will be here this afternoon."

"The journalists," thought Chea. "My friends." His mind raced back to the motel and the hours he used to spend reading their reports. He had told Khom on several occasions that if he decided not to take over his business, he would be very proud if he became a journalist.

"They will help," thought Chea. Newspaper headlines flashed in front of him. CAMBODIA RAVAGED BY COMMUNISTS. UNITED NATIONS CALLS FOR ACTION TO DEMANDS OF WORLD PRESS.

"They will come, as in Israel and Korea," thought Chea. His companion and the other man were now in animated conversation, but they stopped talking as Chea began to pluck at his companion's shirt. They looked at Chea for a moment. His face was gaunt; his eyes were two brown almonds buried in pools of charcoal; bandages covered his elbows and knees. Chea repeated the words, almost in a chant, "The journalists are coming."

"Yes," said the companion with a condescending nod, "yes, the journalists are coming."

"Can I see them, can I see them?" pleaded Chea.

The two men looked at each other and then at Chea. The other one spoke, "Yes, yes, you can see them." His voice indicated that he was trying to get Chea calmed down so that they could go on with the business at hand. "But right now," said the man, "we have to find an English interpreter."

The two got up and were beginning to move away when Chea stood and spoke to them in precise English. "Maybe I can be of service to you."

"Can you really speak English, or is that just one phrase you've learned?"

Chea translated what the man had just said into English and then added, "I have read almost everything the journalists have written about this war."

Each taking an arm, the two men led Chea to a long building that was used for a meeting hall for the camp. Its forty-foot roof was covered with tin. The sides were enclosed with thin U.S. Government plywood, with a three-foot opening at the top for ventilation. It had a wooden floor several feet off the ground to prevent flooding during the afternoon rains. The room was entirely empty. The only light came in from the open space between the roof and the walls.

Chea and three other men sat in a circle in the middle of the room. Several journalists were arriving that day from Bangkok. Each of them tried to impress upon Chea the importance of such a visit. They did not know, nor did Chea tell them, that to have such an encounter was one of the reasons he had escaped from Cambodia. Chea could barely contain his excitement. He sat and listened politely to the men as they gave him advice on how to speak to the journalists, how to answer questions. They did not know that Chea had spent more than one evening sitting beside a pool in a motel near a U.S. air base listening to journalists exchange tales about Asia.

The men were momentarily interrupted as a quiet, self-effacing man, holding his folded hands high on his forehead, made his way through the small door in the side of the room and over to the men. "I have come as you requested," he said timidly, still holding his hands folded in front of his face. He was holding a piece of folded paper in between his hands.

Chea's escort uncrossed his legs, rose, and went over to him. After a brief exchange of words, the escort returned to the circle and the man bowed out the door.

The escort began to unfold the paper and speak at the same time. "One has just come to us from the southern part of our country, from Pineapple Island." Chea knew where it was, at the bottom part of the country, but he had never been there. "We have reports that as many as ten thousand bodies were found there in one village. The man who was just here said he recognized many of the bodies. Here are some of their names."

Chea took the list and his eyes froze on the paper. He began reading names aloud: men he had known or had heard of. It was like walking through a national cemetery and reading the names on the tombs of the famous and near-famous. As Chea read the names, the terrible tiredness began to return.

The heat began to penetrate the small empty building. Chea heard the sound of a car pulling up. The chatter of children greeted the visitors.

"They have arrived," said Chea to no one in particular. Along with his companion and the other man, Chea stood up in the middle of the bare room. The floor shook slightly as several men began to come up the four steps. Four men, all with brown safari suits with short sleeves, followed a soldier.

"I understand you are going to interpret," said the soldier.

"That is correct," said Chea, trying to withhold his excitement. He imagined how his son would look in that kind of a uniform: soldiers in khaki whose weapons were words, not bullets; whose guns were typewriters; who told only truth which in the end always won.

Following the four journalists was the head of the camp. He walked over to Chea, nodded, turned to the journalists, and said in Thai, "Gentlemen, please sit down."

The journalists glanced at each other, looked at the floor, and then awkwardly sat down. The rest squatted or sat in front of them.

The camp commander sat down beside Chea and, while looking at the journalists, told him to interpret loudly and clearly. Chea nodded and said in his most subservient tones, "I will do as you say."

His head was throbbing, and he felt that everyone could see his heart beating beneath the new white shirt that had been loaned to him for the occasion. A new *sampot* covered the wounds on his legs. The sleeves of the shirt covered his bandaged elbows.

"Tell them that this camp has two thousand refugees from almost every part of Cambodia."

Chea repeated the message in English. The journalists all had note pads, but none of them started to write.

"Tell them that when they arrive here they are given food, medicine, shelter, and clothes."

Chea repeated what the camp commander had said. He felt a new sense of confidence, thinking it wasn't as difficult as he had thought it would be. "It would have been easier had the camp commander spoken Cambodian," Chea thought, "but not everyone can speak such a delicate language."

As the report on the camp continued, Chea noticed

that none of the journalists had taken any notes. He had expected that by this time they would painstakingly be writing words that would soon flash around the world.

The camp commander began recounting experiences that different refugees had told about happenings inside Cambodia. Chea had finished translating less than a couple of sentences when one of the journalists raised his hand, smiled benevolently, and began to speak. "I understand," he said in broken English, clearing his throat and beginning again. "We," (emphasizing the *we*, which drew a nod of the head from the other journalists) ". . . we understand that there has been quite a bit of cruelty imposed upon the refugees by the Thai guards . . . is that right?"

The camp commander looked up, stunned. For the first time Chea was aware that the camp commander understood English. Before he could say anything, the camp commander was speaking English, better English than either Chea or the journalist.

"Gentlemen," said the camp commander, "the camp is open for your inspection. You may even live with us, if you desire. We have no secrets."

Another of the journalists, who spoke in very haughty English, something that Chea had never heard before, looked at him and asked a question. "Well, old chap, is it true? How do they abuse you? We understand they take all of your money away as soon as you arrive here."

Chea looked at the camp commander, then at the journalists.

"What about the women that the soldiers mistreat?" said another of the journalists. Now they were all writing.

The fourth journalist, who had not yet spoken, looked at Chea compassionately, and in quite slow tones said, "I note you have fresh bandages under your shirt and I think I also saw one on your leg as you moved. You don't have to be afraid of us; we will protect you. Did they—?"

"Gentlemen," said the camp commander, with a pleading politeness, "this man got those wounds from escaping. He has only been here—"

"Really, old man," interrupted one of the journalists, "really now, we would like to ask them." He pointed to Chea and his two companions. "They are the refugees, you know—not you." Looking at Chea he asked, "How much do they sell the donated rice for? How much do you have to pay for a meal for your family?"

They were still writing.

The camp commander stood up. He put his hands on his hips, stared at the journalists, and without a smile, or anger, said, "Gentlemen of the press, it is too hot in here to continue. Follow me for refreshments." He headed for the door as the four journalists began to get up.

"A hell of a long way to come for some 'refreshment,'" said one of them. As they were leaving the room, two journalists turned to Chea and began to fire questions at him.

"Isn't it true that the Khmer Rouge are really Lon Nol's army trying to get western sympathy?"

"Have you ever seen the Khmer Rouge kill anyone? Do you have any pictures?"

Confusion swept across Chea. It was all wrong. He was the accused. They were the judge and the jury.

"Have you any proof?" demanded the journalist.

"Just as I thought," said the second journalist, "nothing but lies and exaggerations. Anything to get a free bag of rice."

The two men began to leave as Chea remembered

the piece of paper he had in his hand. "Wait!" he cried. "Wait!"

The two journalists stopped near the door and looked back.

"Here!" cried Chea. "Here is your proof. Names of men we have seen dead. Men's names that you can find in your books on our country. Here, read them!"

The journalist who had said the most reached out with a fat, sweaty hand and took the paper. He looked at it for a second and handed it to the other one. After a quick glance, the second journalist handed it back. "A few names, and they call that proof!" The two men turned and went out the door.

Chea could hear one of the journalists say to another: "So there has been a bit of hanky-panky in Cambodia. But a couple of bandages don't tell us much about genocide or the massacres we are supposed to believe."

Chea heard the car door slam and the car drive away. He ran to the door and yelled at the top of his voice after the departing vehicle. "Is beating children to death hanky-panky? Clubbing innocent children to death? And this . . ." Chea pulled his new white shirt off, tearing it in the process. Naked from the waist up, he held up his bandaged arms and yelled at the top of his voice, "And what do you call this? What do you call this?"

Strength drained out of him. His voice broke and he no longer could make anything more than a fractured sound. The crowd that had gathered outside the building looked bewildered and embarrassed. Slowly they began to return to their living quarters.

Chea turned and walked back into the building. He collapsed on the floor and leaned his head against the wall. Tears of frustration ran down his cheeks as he stared at the piece of paper lying on the floor a few feet away. He thought of the names on that piece of paper. He knew there would be no other memorial for those men—only a crumpled piece of paper on the floor of a building in an unmarked refugee camp.

Sweat poured over his chest. "What if Cambodia were Hungary, or Czechoslovakia, or some other European country?" he thought. "Would men who had the ability to dig out facts, to steal classified government documents for the sake of journalistic conscience, ask only a few questions and then dive back into an air-conditioned limousine to head for an air-conditioned bar, leaving the tortured to their torturers?" He was sure that would not be the case. And then another distressing thought came to him. "Maybe the reason the Khmer Rouge were allowed to rape their own nation was because they were Asians, and 'we will just have to let these little yellow men solve their own problems.' The issue isn't political at all," thought Chea, "but a simple case of racism."

His father had taught him, and he in turn had taught his children, that any form of racial prejudice was ungodly. It was a slap against the God who made people with different color skins, different color eyes, different shaped bodies. To hate someone because of that was to hate God.

Chea wasn't sure how long he had sat there. The afternoon sun was disappearing over the tin roofs of the camp when he walked alone down the steps and back to his living quarters. He passed the lines for food. The people pretended they didn't see him as he walked, still bare from the waist up, limping, muttering to himself words that he himself did not even understand. He reached his dorm and threw himself down on his mat, sure of only three things: His son would never become a journalist; he had to get his family out of Cambodia or they would all die; and he was going to have to do it by himself. He only hoped that it would be as easy to get out of the refugee camp as it had been to get in.

Chea's agony of spirit might have been eased somewhat if he could have known that at that very moment, the British correspondent for one of America's most prestigious weekly news magazines was in Hong Kong, writing the final words of a story that depicted with real empathy the carnage rampant in Cambodia. Perhaps that knowledge would have restored Chea's faith in the profession he had once so much desired for his son.

But there was no way for him to know . . . so he lay on his mat—alone with his pain and his God.

TEN

Chea woke, surrounded by darkness. The temperature told him that it was almost morning. His mind was clear again, and he began to plan his return. He had already discussed with several people just where the Thai border was. He had realized, as one helpful soul innocently drew him a map, that he had run so hard during the rain that he had passed the border almost two miles before he arrived at the camp. The problem now was to get out of camp and across the border and river before dawn.

After an hour of planning, he tied three small bags of rice to his *sampot*. He slid silently off his mat and, crouching, went through the doorway. He heard someone snoring, but nothing else. He made his way to the doctor's office and fished out the medicine he had dropped between the slats of the floor.

The thin slice of moon would make no shadows. It would not reveal to others the slight human form that was making its way out of the camp, across the dike, and into the bushes up to the riverbank. "Nature is more consistent than man," he thought. "The moon intends to betray no one. When it shines, it shines; when it doesn't, it doesn't."

The sky was like Chea. It was clear. He saw now,

115

even without the moon. He had another light. In the past several days of crossing mountains, rivers, and other barriers, he had seen a portrait of himself, and he was extremely grateful for it. Like his leg, his spirit still had a long healing process ahead of it. It might never be all that it could be—but it would function. It would carry him, and it could carry others to safety. No army, no matter how cruel or vicious, could stop him. No skeptic could deter him with an army of accusations.

With his self-pity clubbed to death by recent events, his ego bayoneted by the really important issues of the human spirit, he moved cautiously down to the river and began his swim. Either the current had lessened, or he had gained more strength than he had realized. In a short time, he was standing on the other bank. He heard voices. Quickly he slid back into the water. He waited without fear, almost impatiently, as several Khmer soldiers went by. They were making noise, trying to chase away the evil spirits. More and more he was convinced that his country's enemy was more demonic than human. Those young men were controlled by much more than a political ideology. It was at best a facade, a name, an emblem to put on their propaganda. Chea felt certain that the casualties on his side would continue, more of his people would suffer indescribable hardships, but in the end they would conquer.

When the soldiers' voices had faded into the bushes off to the right, Chea headed along the bank parallel to the river and then cut across the small clearing. This time he didn't bother to crawl on his knees. Rather, he crouched down and moved with renewed strength and speed. Originally he had planned only to make it across the river before daylight. Now he could see dawn beginning to break over the hills, and already he was near the road. He headed straight for the mountain peak.

In a few minutes he was crossing the road. He was thankful he hadn't run into the massacred refugees whom he had seen killed three days earlier. The smell of death permeated the otherwise fresh dawn air, so he knew they weren't far away. The smell of death would keep the Khmer Rouge away as well.

The sun was now coming up and he knew he should not attempt to scale the mountain in daylight. He sat down, opened one of the plastic bags of cooked, dried rice, and ate. A large worm wriggled across his foot. He kicked it off and let it go on its way as he put a handful of rice into his mouth. He had been traveling for several hours and was extremely tired. Tonight after dark he would have to climb the mountain and make his way back to his family without being detected. Once he got there, he would have to devise a plan to get them out and across the border.

He went to sleep, too tired to dream. Rain coming down on his face awakened him. It was just beginning to get dark. He looked at the road below. He could see the river and the border. There was no sign of Khmer Rouge soldiers. He lay listening for foreign sounds. There were none. Carefully he crept toward the top of the mountain, moving from one clump of bushes to another.

As the rain continued to fall, he felt mist penetrating the atmosphere. That could mean only one thing. He was getting close to the top of the mountain. He was making better time than he hoped. His strength was beginning to give out, and he sat down to rest. The rain had stopped, and a heavy mist was settling around him. He was again at that point where the clouds "turn in circles." This wasn't the exact spot where he had before spent the night, but it was close. This time, however, it was different. As the mist closed in, laying a blanket of darkness over the valley below and turning the night into a foggy oblivion, he felt refreshed. He didn't feel any of the depression he had felt then. He had more strength and courage than ever before in his life.

Slowly and still cautiously, he began his trip down the side of the mountain. Even in the darkness, it was much easier than the trip up. His major problem was to avoid stumbling over logs left behind by loggers. Soon he was looking into a clearing similar to the one where the Khmer Rouge had cooked the boar. He reached down and felt the sacks of cooked rice attached to a string around his waist. This time he wouldn't have to wait for someone's leftovers. He made his way around the clearing and found himself in the forest. It had taken him two days to travel this far before. He would never know just how much of that time was spent in semiconsciousness or unconsciousness, or how much time he spent going around in circles.

Suddenly Chea saw a clearing ahead, one he hadn't seen on his journey out. He lay down for awhile and waited for the sky to clear and for the moon to come out. He hadn't been there long when his nostrils picked up a pungent odor coming from his right. He recognized it immediately.

It was the graveyard of his own camp. A journey that had taken him three days before had now taken less than four or five hours. He was amazed he hadn't been caught.

He moved back a few yards and settled down in one of the clumps of bushes he had facetiously begun calling "motels." He lay for several minutes studying the terrain. Little lights flickered in front of him, perhaps the fireflies which often came out after the rains. When they didn't move, it dawned on him with exultation that he was watching the fires from his own camp. The old people were cooking the evening meal. The desire to crawl down into the camp and search out his wife was a great temptation, but he realized the risk involved—not only for himself, but for others as well. He couldn't see any soldiers. The bushes where the Supervisor stayed were out of sight around the corner.

Chea gazed from fire to fire. Which one belonged to his family? He thought he might have it located, but he couldn't be sure. Looking at the lights, he became pensive. How many fires like these were burning in Cambodia tonight? How many families were gathering around their fires to cook their few grams of rice? How many fires were lighting small clearings while the stench of dead loved ones rode the wind into camp, a constant reminder that even if these people were freed tomorrow a part of them would remain in this desolate spot that had witnessed so much treachery? Chea looked at the trees that had observed wild life, predatory animals, for centuries. Surely even they stood back in revulsion at the starvation, beatings, stabbings, shootings, burials.

He wondered if he were not as much to blame as any one else. It was easy for him to blame foreign journalists, but what had caused the story to develop in such a way that the journalists didn't want to report or even believe it? How many Smiling Ones had passed through his Sunday school class over the years but tonight were carrying clubs and AK-17 automatic rifles?

He slept, and again daylight came. He strained his eyes to look. The graveyard had invaded the camp so far, he couldn't imagine many villagers being alive unless more citizen prisoners had been brought in. He looked from hut to hut. He thought he saw his. In a few minutes, his doubt was dispelled. A young boy, with Khom's walk, moved from around the hut, picked up a shovel, and walked slowly to the graveyard for his daily task of digging shallow graves. Chea's eyes moved over there. He tried to see his own grave, but the area had expanded on all sides. It was impossible to locate either his or his daughter's.

Khom made his way across the piles of leaves, chasing off a few rats with his shovel, then disappeared from sight.

Chea turned his attention back to the hut, waiting for a sight of Kolab. She would have to come out shortly. Other women were beginning to move toward the trees where they gathered their roots, berries, and leaves. Still no sign of her.

Then to his left he saw a woman approaching with a baby tied to her back. His heart leapt. He was sure it was Kolab, carrying Baby Sister. But wait, she looked too stooped. Her hair was too disheveled. She walked with a decided limp. But yes, yes, it was Kolab and Baby Sister. The last old woman in the unit must have died, so Kolab had to carry the child to work with her. He watched as the woman, bent and limping, reached her work area near the forest. She untied the cloth around her chest and set the baby on the ground. The baby didn't move. Oh, that couldn't be Baby Sister. She would be up and running around by then. Then he saw the woman's face.

Even from that distance, Kolab looked thin and haggard. Chea's heart burned within him. More than anything else he wanted to run to her, put his arms around her, and lead her into the jungle. To do so would be death for both of them. He lay watching as she worked pulling roots. His heart ached to help her. Hours went by. No soldier appeared. But he couldn't take the chance of getting her attention.

It distressed him to see Baby Sister just lying in the shade, still not moving. He guessed that camp conditions had worsened after he left, that everyone was near the end of physical endurance. Across the camp he could see only four or five men working. Were they all that were left? Had all the rest died? Had they tried to escape and been killed?

Scanning the camp, he noticed the women preparing to return to their huts. It must be near 11:00 A.M., time for the midday meal. The longest morning in Chea's lifetime had passed.

Kolab dropped the bark she was stripping and wrapped the cloth around her chest. She picked up Baby Sister, put her on her stooped back, and began to hobble home.

Chea had to make contact. He had to get them out of there. But how? He looked at the spot where she was working. He had to take the chance. The guards usually walked through the camp at the meal break to make sure everyone had returned.

He crawled on his stomach, pulling himself with his elbows. One of his bandages came off, but he didn't care. He had to move fast while everyone was eating. He watched for soldiers. Sweating, straining, he finally crawled to a place directly behind the tree from which Kolab had been pulling off pieces of bark. He could only hope that she would return to the same place and finish her job of stripping bark this afternoon. Without rising, he reached into the tuck of his *sampot* and pulled out the banana leaf. As gently as always, he unwrapped it and took out the white scarf. He reached out and found a smaller leaf. He felt around for a small vine and broke off a piece no larger than a match. Using his tumbnail to sharpen the end, he used the bit of wood to punch out little holes that read "Bring family here." He prayed that Kolab would understand. He put the leaf inside the scarf, folded it, and gently replaced it in the banana leaf, wrapping it with new grass.

Now he had to get it to her. Keeping his head to the ground he focused on the piece of bark she had pulled from the tree. Not daring to lift his head, he quickly tossed the little package over to the piece of bark where she had last been working. It landed right on top! She couldn't miss it. He crawled backward inch by inch, taking a deep breath only when he was back in his bush-motel.

It was beginning to cloud up; the afternoon rains would soon pay their daily visit. The women should be returning to the field any moment. What if they had changed the afternoon schedule? Kolab looked so tired this morning, maybe she wouldn't make it back to the forest.

His fears were cut short when he saw Khom repeat the morning walk to the graveyard. Women began to make their way to the edge of the forest, while the few men headed in the opposite direction. Kolab came walking out of the hut, again with Baby Sister tied to her back. Her limp looked more decided. Chea watched her every step, fearful that she might change her course and head to another part of the clearing. She didn't. She went directly back to where she had been that morning, setting Baby Sister down not far from the torn-off bark.

"Look at it," Chea whispered to himself. "Look at it, it's right in front of you."

Baby Sister stayed on the ground in the shade while Kolab tore off more bark, throwing it in a pile. One piece landed right on top of the wrapped leaves.

Chea's heart sank. What would he do now? She would pick up the bark and carry it to the camp, probably losing the wrapped leaves, the scarf, and the message in the process. A movement caught Chea's eye. Baby Sister was now in the sun. For the first time, she moved on her own, crawling into a shady spot near the note.

"Please, Baby Sister, be your old self and play with the bark," Chea pleaded silently.

Baby Sister just lay there.

Having taken all the bark from the tree, Kolab walked a little farther into the forest looking for berries. Some minutes later she returned and deposited a few berries on top of the bark. Baby Sister moved toward them. She crawled to the bark and one by one popped the berries into her mouth. Those caught eating food outside the allotted time suffered serious consequences. But right now Chea worried only about whether or not she would notice the note under the berries. Baby Sister took a piece of bark and held it across her lap, exposing the folded leaves. Chea could hardly contain himself. The little package was in full view, but Kolab had gone after more berries.

Then it happened. Baby Sister saw the green leaves. "Maybe she thinks they're food," thought Chea. Baby Sister listlessly took the leaves in her hands. Just then Kolab came back with more berries. She immediately scolded Baby Sister for eating the others. Chea froze. Kolab stopped and stared at Baby Sister. Chea was afraid to breathe.

Kolab took the leaves from Baby Sister's hands. She looked from side to side. There were no soldiers. Picking up a piece of bark and pretending to break it, she broke the grass around the leaves. She saw the white scarf. For the first time she knew that not only was Chea alive, but he had come back for them. She took the leaf out of the scarf, read the message, then looked toward the forest. Chea could see the disbelief on her face. She tore up the leaf and tucked the scarf into the fold of her torn, dirty *sampot*. She looked again into the forest where she thought her husband must be hiding. She was looking in the wrong direction, but Chea could see that Kolab's face was wreathed in a smile. Her beauty had returned. She pointed her finger in a downward motion. "Here. We'll meet you here."

She returned to work, fervently pulling bark from the trees. Chea thought he heard her singing.

A few hours later Kolab strapped Baby Sister to her back, and her shoulders high, she headed for her hut. She stumbled, and then slowed her stride, being more careful. Khom was returning from the graveyard at the same time, and Kolab took his arm and led him inside the hut.

Again Chea waited. The rains started again as darkness descended. He prayed that it would rain harder than it had ever rained before. It was already raining hard enough to hide their escape. There could be no fires outside, and the soldiers would expect everyone to be in their hut.

Chea waited, watched, waited, watched. Nothing. The rains came and went. The sky cleared, and he could see the fires being lit. His heart sank as he saw one in front of his hut come to life. They couldn't make it tonight. Maybe there was a meeting after supper. Any number of reasons could keep them from leaving.

"Chea."

He was sure he heard it. He held his breath.

"Chea, Chea Aim. Chea Aim."

Only Kolab called him by his full name. He turned on his stomach, trying to locate the sound.

"Coming. Coming," he answered, crawling in the direction of the sound as fast as he elbows would pull him.

"Chea." The voice was nearer.

"Kolab, my Kolab," he whispered.

He located the sound. It was coming from a clump of bushes nearer the graveyard. He crawled there as fast as he could. He moved under the bush and saw them lying there. Kolab, Khom, and Baby Sister. He crawled over and wrapped Kolab in his arms. "Kolab, my Kolab. I'm back, I'm back."

She began quietly weeping. "I was afraid you couldn't come," she said between sobs.

Beside her was Khom. Chea moved apprehensively over to him. Khom fell into his arms, burying his face in his father's neck. "I'm sorry, Father. I'm sorry." In the second of time before their embrace, Chea caught a glimpse of something white around Khom's neck. He knew what it was. Holding him close, Chea felt the white ivory dove around his son's neck rub against his own white cross.

Chea gently moved Khom to one side. There, lying on the ground, was Baby Sister. One look told Chea that she was very ill.

"She has been very sick," said Kolab. "Right after you died—left, she got dysentery. She still can't eat."

Chea picked up his little jewel. The sparkle was gone. His joy at holding her in his arms was tempered by his apprehension.

The moon was now shining through the clouds, and suddenly Chea realized how exposed they were to the soldiers. Without saying a word, Chea held onto Baby Sister and slid on his side across the wet grass, heading for the forest. Kolab and Khom followed in the same position. Finally they were surrounded by trees. Chea stood cautiously and looked back toward the camp. He could see nothing. Holding Baby Sister, he began to walk. The others followed.

"We will travel farther and then stop for something to eat. We must be deep in the forest by morning when they find that you are gone."

Chea hadn't noticed how exhausted Kolab and Khom had gotten. The excitement and tension of the initial escape had worn off, their adrenaline had gone back to normal, and their weakened bodies began to give out.

Chea sat down beside several big trees and took his last bag of cooked rice from his belt. He handed it to his son who, in turn, pointed to Baby Sister. She needed it more than anyone else. Chea put some in the palm of his hand and took Baby Sister in his arms. He tried to force some of the rice through her parched lips. She opened her eyes and looked at him, but she didn't respond to the food.

A sting penetrated Chea's breast as he looked into her face. Fear and love enmeshed themselves in his heart as he dropped the rice into her mouth, holding her close, and murmuring words that only she could hear.

After a short rest, they began moving again. It was now possible to walk upright. Chea headed for what he was sure was the clearing where he'd seen the soldiers the first time.

"I can't go on," murmured Kolab. "Go without me. Save the children," she pleaded as she again lay on the ground.

"It is for you that I have returned," said Chea tenderly. "For you, and for them. We will go on together as a family, or we will not go on at all."

Chea could see that it was painful for Kolab to get up. Her legs were swollen, and her stomach distended. She was suffering from malnutrition more than the others. Chea was certain that her food had been going to the children while she herself slowly starved.

Ahead, through the trees, Chea saw one of his bush-motels. He took Kolab's hand and led her under the bushes. "We'll rest her until dawn, and then move on."

Everyone lay down, not speaking. The meeting near the graveyard had washed away any animosity between Khom and Chea. Kolab would never again be Wife; now she was a person with a name. There was no need to rehearse the past, but to plan for the future.

Chea broke the silence. "I was afraid you wouldn't come tonight. I don't think I could have spent another night being so close to you and yet so far. I'm afraid I would have crawled to you."

"We had to leave tonight or never," Kolab said as she reached over and took his hand. "They were going to send the women and children away tomorrow. It was our last night in camp."

Gratitude overflowed from Chea's heart as he realized the perfect timing. "What about the men? What are they going to do with them?"

"The Stranger came a couple of days ago. He looked at the cornfield. When he dug up the dirt they say he found very little corn beginning to sprout. Everyone who planted it was killed. Only six men remain."

Anger welled up in Chea. He wished those journalists were with him now. His anger began to spread across the world, to the United Nations, to America, to Hanoi, and to Peking, where his Prince was evidently living in the luxury of exile. And then a warm feeling came over his spirit, and his pity moved from those men who had been clubbed to death to those who were sitting in cocktail lounges in Bangkok solving the world's problems to those who were in their chauffeur-driven limousines making their way to places at a horseshoe table along the Hudson River in New York. He realized that at this exact moment in history there was no other person in the world that he would want to be. He wouldn't trade his wet place under a dripping bush for the finest hotel suite in Bangkok.

His euphoria was interrupted by a sound he had heard many times before. This time it was barely audible. "Da Da."

Chea, Kolab, and Khom all turned to Baby Sister. She had spoken for the first time since he had returned. He cradled her in his arms. Khom reached over and stroked her spindly leg, which was now hardly big enough to hold the sores that covered it. Kolab gently stroked her forehead.

Chea was just opening his mouth to speak when she opened her eyes. He saw the sparkle and knew the little jewel was back. A tiny smile came across her swollen, cracked lips. She whispered, "Daddy's home," and then went limp in Chea's arms.

As dawn was breaking, the remaining three turned away from the small mound of leaves under the bush. Khom had made a cross from a couple of twigs and put it at one end. They had used up all the tears they had. Now all they could do was crawl away and try not to look back. "Someday," said Chea, "we will meet our little jewel again."

It was a long morning. Chea found that boys are much more adept at catching food in the forest than their fathers. When Khom appeared with three small lizards by the tail, Chea thought that they looked much more appetizing than worms and bark.

They circled the clearing, hoping to reach the top of the mountain by nightfall. If their endurance held out, they could be across the border by tomorrow.

Kolab's strength was ebbing fast for lack of nourishment. Chea found a spot where they could rest and motioned for Khom to go around to the back of the bushes. Chea sat down beside Kolab and took her tiny, thin fingers in his hand. She opened her eyes and smiled. "You won't leave me, will you?"

Chea smiled back. "Only if you refuse to eat your dinner."

Khom appeared from behind the bushes with three pieces of meat, tailless, legless, headless. Chea didn't know how he had done it, but he wasn't about to question the chef. Satisfaction was written on Khom's face. With no more ado, he handed the meat to his father and mother. Kolab pursed her lips and held it aside for a moment.

Chea held his up and said, "Here's my fuel for climbing the mountain," and dropped it into his mouth. With only a little coughing, the meat disappeared. In a few seconds the other two did the same, and then they all laughed.

Traveling again, they were moving faster than they had anticipated. The delicacies that Khom picked up along the way—berries, roots, and a few little animals that couldn't move as fast as a twelve-year-old boy—supplied the energy. The rains came in the afternoon, though with less severity now, and just as it was getting dark, the three reached the mountaintop.

Huddling together in the cold of night. More of Khom's delicacies. Cut feet. Smell of dead bodies. Scraped arms from crawling. A near broken leg from falling in a ditch. A close brush with some Khmer Rouge soldiers. Swimming a shallow river.

Chea Aim and his family could see the lights of the refugee camp at last. The three lay in one of the bushes that Chea had used on his last trip. This time he had his precious jewels with him. He was a completed man. He explained the irrigation ditch, the rumor that there were mine fields, and that the Khmer Rouge liked refugee target practice. He knew now that just across the irrigation ditch and about 500 yards to the north there was a Thai police station. Khmer Rouge would probably be there as well, so he decided to take the same route as before. But tonight the rain had stopped and the moon was shining across the clearing. No clouds were in sight.

He was about to move out when his wife grabbed his arm and pointed. Silhouetted against the sky were five Khmer Rouge soldiers, walking across their escape route.

Chea and his family hugged the ground. The ugly fear that Chea had come to hate began to creep across his mind. He laid his head on the ground for a minute, spoke gently to himself, and then whispered to his family. "We'll wait here until they pass by."

The three of them lay with their faces in the dirt. Then Chea slowly lifted his head and looked in the direction where he had seen the soldiers. He strained to see. The moon kept appearing and then disappearing behind the clouds. "They could be sitting down eating their supper," he said as he tried to scan the entire escape route. "I can't see anyone." He lifted himself up cautiously on his elbows. His head froze in one position, a bit to his right. "I see it," he said excitedly.

Khom began to rise up as well.

"Down, keep your head down," Chea warned. Khom immediately dropped back.

Chea laid his head on the ground facing his wife and son. "I see the light of the Thai border police stations."

"How far?" asked Khom excitedly, moving his body up a little and then settling on the ground again as he looked at his father.

"Just a little to the right, and not too far. I think we can make it. But first we're going to have to move over so that we'll be straight across from the lights and away from the soldiers."

"Why don't we run for it?" asked Khom.

"Not yet," warned Chea. "It will come to that, but not yet. We'll have to crawl for awhile first." His voice trailed off as he squeezed his wife's hand and then pivoted around on his stomach. Khom and Kolab repeated Chea's action and the three began to crawl on their bellies.

"I'm not sure my elbows will carry me anymore," said Kolab.

Chea turned his head and noticed his wife's elbows

were bleeding. Her face was buried in the grass and dirt. Digging his toes into the ground, he slid back beside her. He placed his arm around her and could feel her back heaving. He moved his head over and whispered into her ear. "We'll make it. Only a little way. We'll make it."

She turned her head. He reached over and wiped the dirt and grass from her face. Tears had turned the dirt to little drops of clay. Chea felt a lump in his throat as he realized that she had been crying for some time. As he kissed her gently below each eye, he tasted the tears and dirt.

The fear of the enemy out in the darkness disappeared. "We're going to make a run for it," he said. "If we die, we die together."

In a second, all three were on their feet. Then, just as the moon went behind a cloud, they saw the lights, straight in front of them.

"Let's go!" urged Chea.

The family took each other's hands and, crouching, started to run.

The lights grew closer. All three were breathing heavily. Kolab fell once, but Chea and Khom held her hands and half carried her between them.

Chea thought he heard someone yell. Then a sound that he could not mistake caused all three to fall to the ground. Bullets whined over their heads, and little pops of dirt began to explode around them.

In other times Chea might have had to spend precious seconds analyzing what to do next. He would have weighed the terms of survival. But not anymore. "I'll count to three," said Chea, not bothering to whisper. "On three we'll all jump and run, straight ahead. Straight ahead."

His voice was interrupted as a flare exploded, blinding them and bathing them in a sea of light.

"Three!" The family started running. Bullets began to fly in their direction. Chea heard one zing just over his head.

"Run, run, don't look back!" he shouted. Then he made a quick turn to his right. He headed in the direction of the soldiers. He waved his arms to make sure they saw him. "Here I am! Here I am!" he yelled.

Kolab fell in total exhaustion with Khom by her side. A Thai policeman knelt beside her.

"We made it," said Khom, putting his hands to his chest to ease the pain.

"Yes," whispered Kolab. Then they heard a sound overriding the gunfire. They had never heard an exploding land mine before. Kolab's hand came up to her mouth. The little piece of white material she was holding stifled her moan.

In the momentary light of the exploding land mine they saw a man being lifted in the air, his arms outstretched in a sacrificial silhouette.

Silence came over the land. The rest of the world rolled over to catch a few more minutes' sleep.

POSTSCRIPT
by Dr. Robert H. Bowman

As president and one of the founders of the Far East Broadcasting Company, I am often asked what appears to be a rather simple question: What is FEBC? In many cases I give them some statistics, maybe a piece of literature, and we go our separate ways. Then I reflect on the question myself. What is the Far East Broadcasting Company?

The question begins to stir in me something that lies below the surface of simple answers. The words probe the past, the past comes to life, and I begin to marvel at what God has done.

It is during these very personal times that I begin to think of FEBC as a network, not of radio stations, but of almost invisible threads which extend from such places as Manila, Bangalore, Tokyo, Seoul, San Francisco, and other famous cities printed boldly on tourist maps. These threads reach out into areas which we usually associate with famine, strife, war, materialism, and other tragic world problems.

Then, almost afraid to move, I reach down and gently tug on one of these threads. Over there, hundreds, maybe thousands of miles away, a tiny speck moves. As I look I expect to see fear and anguish and hate, but instead there is a smile. I see a person. True, he may be wearing clothes made in Paris, or tied together with twine. His stomach may be extended from too much food, or distended by not having enough, but the smile is real. These are the men, women, and children that God has reached out and touched through the spoken word of the Far East Broadcasting Company. These are the unnumbered that God has reached out and knotted to our message and Messenger.

I remember so well that day, over thirty years ago, when we tossed out our first thread. It was just a small radio station, in Manila, Philippines. The future wasn't very bright. The city was a pile of ashes, just now cooling enough so that the people could begin to probe the pile of rubble for the remains of loved ones, and to build a new nation. MacArthur had returned, and had gone...all the way north. "It's too early. The people are too busy rebuilding their nation," said our friends. "This nation will never recover. And look, only a few government officials have radios—it won't work," warned the experts. Last summer I was in Manila, and I stood beside the President of that great country. The ashes have turned to some of Asia's most beautiful buildings. Together we pulled those little threads, and everywhere people stood and smiled and applauded and said, "Thank you, Mr. Bowman, for coming to Manila, not just now when everything is so comfortable, but in those days when you ducked between cobras and Communist guerrillas to build that first radio station."

And then there was China. The people had just been "liberated" by a man called Mao. "But there are too many of them. They want nothing to do with colonialism, what Christianity is associated with. The opium war, the Boxer rebellion, extraterritorial rights—you know, this is a different age," said our friends. "They have no radios," the experts advised. But there was something else they did not have—Jesus Christ.

Recently I gently tugged on another little thread, and the beautiful harbor of Hong Kong rustled. There was a smiling face. Again this one was lined with fear stamped on by a lifetime in a police state. I saw a slim body shivering after a long swim through shark-infested, freezing waters. The smile warmed me. As the young man told of listening to FEBC so many years, he spoke quietly, intensely. "It was our only contact with the gospel," he said. "We copied down the Scripture as you dictated it to us. We risked seven years in prison to listen to you. But we listened, we wrote, and then we carried the Scripture a page at a time to our friends." He is one of the 900 million.

When FEBC was being born, a little boy in a small nation off the coast of Florida was involved in the mischief of little boys all over the world. As we both grew, FEBC had the opportunity to purchase a station in San Francisco to broadcast to Latin America.

"Latin America is lost. Forget it," said our friends. "Broadcasting from America, you will be just a Yankee imperialist. Besides, no one is sure that the masses have radios," warned the experts.

The little boy became Fidel Castro, and his mischief became revolution. And KGEI became the Latin American Service of the Far East Broadcasting Company.

One day I gently tugged on another of those threads. Someone turned and looked at me. There was that smile again. A young man who had been a disciple of Fidel Castro, a regular listener to Radio Havana. One day he heard a different message, coming from San Francisco, California. As he listened, the message and the Messenger took over his life. He didn't have to say anything. He just smiled, and as he walked away we saw the Russian rifle thrown aside to rust alone in the jungle. The hand grenades lay in some leaves, where the jungle would claim them, unexploded, to be dug up some day by an archaeologist, to perplex the geniuses of this world. At the end of the thread a young man walks, head up, no fear, a Bible under his arm, to the nation of Peru just outside the clearing.

The Far East Broadcasting Company...what is it? True, it is twenty-eight radio stations, located in Manila, Korea, Saipan, and San Francisco. These transmitters do broadcast 2,100 hours per week, in seventy-two different languages with programs produced in studios located in such places as Tokyo, Seoul, Hong Kong, Singapore, Bangalore, and New Delhi and other major cities in the world. Six hundred people run transmitters, write scripts, and answer the 30,000 letters we receive each month. Those are more than statistics. FEBC is people and a Person. FEBC is God's continuing miracle of missionary radio. FEBC is part of the body of Jesus Christ. FEBC is a vast network of almost invisible threads reaching out to places and people we have never heard of...at least not yet. The other day, I pulled ever so gently on this thread and it reached into Cambodia. You know what "friends" and "experts" have to say. But we know better, and so do all the Chea Aims who survived.